MUSIC FOR LIFE

Fiona Maddocks is the classical music critic of the *Observer*. She was founder editor of *BBC Music Magazine* and chief arts feature writer for the *London Evening Standard*, and is the author of *Hildegard of Bingen: The Woman of Her Age* (Faber) and *Harrison Birtwistle: Wild Tracks – A Conversation Diary* (Faber).

Fiona Maddocks

MUSIC
for LIFE

100 Works to Carry
You Through

FABER & FABER

First published in 2016
by Faber & Faber Limited
Bloomsbury House
74–77 Great Russell Street
London WC1B 3DA

Typeset by Faber & Faber Limited
Printed and bound by CPI Group (UK) Ltd, Croydon, CR0 4YY

A CIP record for this book
is available from the British Library

ISBN 978-0-571-32938-0

MIX
Paper from
responsible sources
FSC® C020471

2 4 6 8 10 9 7 5 3 1

For my father
and the memory of my mother

Contents

Introduction

The Starting Point

In compiling a list of this kind, I had one rule: the music comes first. I have always resisted the idea of expecting music to feed or prompt an emotional state, so I tried to ask the question the other way round. Why do I want to listen to a particular work at any given moment? What is the imperative? Beethoven's 'Hammerklavier' Sonata was the name of the first piece I wrote down. Soon I had a couple of hundred absolute dead certainties and a mild sense of panic.

The categories came later, a broad and flexible way of ordering choices. Numerous works can appear under several headings. I realise this. So will the reader.

To help narrow the field, I laid down a few guidelines: no operas, as they have their own narrative already (though one or two overtures have crept in). No song cycles for the same reason, though they too slip in surreptitiously. Rather than omit the entire, rich treasury of Lieder, I have dropped a song into most sections, a change of pace and scale.

No one needs musical knowledge to read this book. There are pointers for those who want to dig deeper. All the music is easy to sample online so you can hear and read together, apart, before, after. Suggested recordings appear at the end.

These are my own preferences, so let's not talk about balance. They range from the well known to the unfamiliar.

They are, with exceptions where the choice is part of a bigger enterprise, complete works for any forces. Early and Renaissance composers wrote much of their work for the church; broadly speaking this, mainly, is what has survived. I would have liked to include more from this period, but not everyone (I'm told) wants a long list of masses. Baroque, too, would have been easier had I allowed myself a few Handel operas or more Bach (see below). I steered away from an overdose of symphonies – they too warrant separate attention – though broke that rule too. With contemporary composers I imposed a limit: only those born before 1940 (with one short-lived exception in Claude Vivier). I could as happily limit myself to include only those born after that date. Another list, another book.

Many works, their composers, their lovers, their stories, spill across each other. If this were online, the text would be pitted with embedded links. I have left those overlaps to the readers, without annotation, so they can adopt that quaint old habit of stumbling across connections for themselves.

The Omissions

No selection such as this can be 'right'. Omissions will be shouted down, eccentric inclusions pilloried. No Dvořák, no Prokofiev, no Philip Glass – though they all get mentioned in dispatches, and in the index. Lists of best-known masterpieces are easy to find elsewhere, if that's what you are after. Online playlists deal with every mood and need (music to cry, sleep, hoover, eat to).

Many of the greatest works in the canon defy this sort of categorisation. 'These are the Alps. What is there to say about them?' as Basil Bunting characterised Ezra Pound's *Cantos*. The symphonies of Haydn, Mozart, Beethoven, Brahms, Schumann, Bruckner, Mahler, Sibelius, Shostakovich, as a start, should be in every library. A few are here. Johann Sebastian Bach is a continent apart. Could music lovers survive without the *B minor Mass*, the *St Matthew Passion*, the *St John Passion*, the cantatas, the motets, the *Goldberg Variations*, the *Musical Offering*, the organ chorale preludes, the French and English keyboard suites, the sonatas and partitas for solo violin and the suites for solo cello, the *Brandenburg Concertos*?

If there is an emphasis on chamber and piano music, it reflects my interests, as well as a preference for smaller works for private listening. We cannot all get to concert halls but, given the chance, they surely remain the best places to hear big symphonies or to meet new repertoire for the first time. Some of this music has taken a long time to work its way into my bloodstream. There's no equivalent to speed-reading (or speed-dating for that matter) with the great works of the repertoire.

A short overview at the end of each section indicates some other works you might have expected to find but haven't – or that, after much heated debate with myself, fell into oblivion. These round-ups are intended not only to save my skin but to suggest further exploration. Pictures offer an accompanying dialogue, some literal in reference, others evocative. The book is offered in the hope of sharing music that, together with those great summits mentioned above, sustains me. It is a compendium but the lid is open. Throw out and renew as you like. If you feel moved to count, you will find that there are in fact over a hundred. My justification is that by the time you have crossed out the ones that do not speak to you, you might still secure the nominated century. This is today's list. Yesterday's or tomorrow's? Another matter entirely.

1

CHILDHOOD, YOUTH

The first blossom was the best blossom
For the child who never had seen an orchard;
For the youth whom whisky had led astray
The morning after was the first day.

LOUIS MACNEICE, 'Apple Blossom'

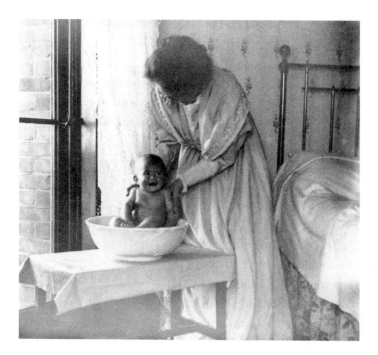

PÉROTIN

Alleluia nativitas (*c.* 1200)

Where better to start a book about music's importance for life than with a nativity? Little is known about Pérotin. His birth date is uncertain. He died around 1226. He was active in Paris at the turn of the twelfth century, when the great Gothic cathedral of Notre Dame, on the Île de la Cité, was under construction. In that distant time, nearly every artist – composer or painter, stonemason or architect – was unknown, and working, as they believed, for the glory of God. Pérotin is among the first we can identify, there at the dawn of Western music. We know of him thanks to a treatise dating from the thirteenth century by an English writer – perhaps a travelling scholar at the University of Paris. The document, and sometimes the writer, are referred to as Anonymous IV. Copies were found in the cathedral of Bury St Edmunds, Suffolk, and eventually published in the nineteenth century. Pérotin's three-part motet *Alleluia nativitas* was written for the feast day of the Virgin Mary. The three voice parts dance together in different short, rhythmic patterns and varying phrase lengths, uniting in a single line of chant, overlapping in consonance and dissonance. The effect is sprung and vital, haunting and unearthly.

WOLFGANG AMADEUS MOZART

Twelve Variations on 'Ah vous dirai-je, Maman' (1781–2)

In fact and in legend Wolfgang Amadeus Mozart is still the crown prince of musical prodigies. His earliest pieces, written down by his proud father Leopold (whom today we might call a Tiger Dad), date from when Mozart was aged four or five. These variations for piano, by comparison, are the work of a well-established young composer of twenty-five, having gleeful fun with a childhood song. The playfulness with which he adorns the French nursery rhyme 'Ah vous dirai-je, Maman' ('Oh shall I tell you, Mama') is evident from the solemn simplicity of the opening theme to the growing complexity as Mozart moves from rapid quavers, to lilting triplets, to busy semiquavers, now in the right hand, now in the left, with crisp ornament and abundant, run-around pleasure. The song was popular in the eighteenth century and also used for 'Twinkle, Twinkle, Little Star', 'Baa, Baa, Black Sheep' and other nursery songs and carols. Liszt, Dohnányi and Saint-Saëns (in *The Carnival of the Animals*) also made use of it. Tchaikovsky orchestrated his own, just recognisable version in his Orchestral Suite No. 4, *Mozartiana* (1887), a centenary tribute to Mozart's opera *Don Giovanni*. Out of an unpromising scrap came a sparkling gem.

ROBERT SCHUMANN

Abegg Variations (1831)

How does a composer decide he or she is ready to face the world with the naming of an opus 1? Robert Schumann's wife Clara, also a composer, started precociously with Four Polonaises in 1831, when she was eleven. Schumann was slower. He began his career with some confusion, first studying law then abandoning it for art – but which art, poetry or music? Eventually in 1831 – by coincidence the same year as Clara, his new piano pupil and nine years his junior – Schumann took the leap with his *Variations on the Name 'Abegg'*. He was twenty-one. This challenging and vir-tuosic work became his Op. 1. He dedicated it to 'Pauline, Countess of Abegg', probably a friend from his youth, whose name cried out for musical invention, with a theme on the notes A–B–E–G–G. The critic of the *Wiener Zeitung* gave it a perceptive review: 'The probably still youthful composer, whom we have never encountered before, is a rare phenome-non of our age: he follows no school, draws his ideas from his own mind, and declines to preen himself with . . . borrowed plumes. He has created an ideal world in which he gambols with almost reckless abandon, at times even with original bizarrerie . . .' If only all of us, assessing new talent, could be so accurate.

GEORGES BIZET

Jeux d'enfants (1871)

Georges Bizet's life was colourful and short. The son of a wigmaker father and musician mother, he wrote a sparkling Symphony in C major at the age of seventeen. Aware of his own facility, he once said he wanted to do nothing 'chic', an adjective less talented composers might quite enjoy having applied to their work. These dozen pieces for piano duet were written near the end of his brief career, a few months before the birth of his only child; they are of varying levels of difficulty (but easier than many of Bizet's keyboard works). They conjure childhood games as if straight from the toy box itself. Each title requires no explanation: 'The Swing', 'The Top', 'The Doll', 'Wooden Horses', 'Battledore and Shuttlecock', 'Trumpet and Drum', 'Soap Bubbles', 'Puss in the Corner', 'Blind Man's Buff', 'Leapfrog', 'Little Husband, Little Wife', 'The Ball'. Bizet orchestrated five movements and named them *Petite Suite*, from which Georges Balanchine made a ballet. Crisp and witty, *Jeux d'enfants* acted as a prototype for other French composers – for Fauré in his *Dolly Suite*, and Ravel in *Ma mère l'Oye*, both also for piano duet, and for Debussy in his *Children's Corner* for solo piano. All this music of childhood, including Schumann's *Kinderszenen* as well, sounds temptingly easy to play, yet has fiendish, finger-tripping traps at every turn: the nursery reimagined through infant memories rewoven in adulthood.

FELIX MENDELSSOHN

Octet (1825)

Irresistible and irrepressible, Mendelssohn's Octet has no fault, no weakness and a confidence instantly recognisable as the voice of this composer. A string player himself, Felix Mendelssohn (1809–1847) wrote his Octet for double string quartet – four violins, two violas, two cellos – when he was sixteen. He wanted it to be 'played by all the instruments in the style of a symphony'. Mendelssohn's sister and fellow composer Fanny gives a vivid description of the *Scherzo*, saying that her brother told her that he had set the 'Walpurgis Night Dream' from Goethe's *Faust*: 'The flight of the clouds and the veil of mist/Are lighted from above.' Fanny continues: 'The whole piece is to be played staccato and pianissimo . . . the trills passing away with the quickness of lightning . . . One feels so near the world of spirits, carried away in the air, half inclined to snatch up the broomstick and follow the aerial procession. At the end the first violinist takes flight with a feather-like lightness, and – all has vanished.' For the players there is no let-up: the music spits and sparkles, flickers and quivers from part to capricious part. Every player must hang on for dear life and count like a demon. One falter, and this perfect edifice can collapse in an ungainly heap (speaking from bitter, though fortunately private, experience).

Piano Concerto No. 1 in F sharp minor (1891)

Kick-starting his career with an apparent blaze of confidence, Rachmaninoff wrote the first of his four piano concertos in 1891 when still a student. He told a friend he was pleased with his efforts. Nothing is ever straightforward with Rachmaninoff. He had already attempted writing a piano concerto two years earlier, but had abandoned it. He was not a model student, needing much coercion to get his work done, though eventually he secured a coveted Great Gold Medal at the Moscow Conservatory. Despite his initial pride, Rachmaninoff then hid the piece from sight. In 1908 he suggested, with muted enthusiasm, that he might rework it: 'Of course it will have to be written all over again, for its orchestration is worse than its music.' In 1917 he eventually completed the task, and was himself soloist in the first performance in 1919 at Carnegie Hall, New York. By 1931, now in his late fifties, he was still bothered: 'I look at my early works and see how much there is that is superfluous . . . I have rewritten my First Concerto; it is really good now. All the youthful freshness is there, and yet it plays itself so much more easily. And nobody pays any attention. When I tell them in America that I will play the First Concerto, they do not protest but I can see by their faces that they would prefer the Second or Third . . . It is incredible how many stupid things I did at the age of nineteen. All composers do it.' Up to a point, and not half as well.

CLAUDE VIVIER

Lonely Child (1980)

'Not knowing my parents enabled me to create a magnificent dream world. I shaped my origins exactly as I wished,'
the French-Canadian composer Claude Vivier (1948–1983),
not in any circles a household name, once said. Does it make
a difference to know the circumstances in which music is
written? In this case, yes. Vivier, born in Montreal, studying with Stockhausen then making his home in Paris, was
abandoned at birth. Brought up by nuns in a children's home
before being adopted at three, he invested his music with a
sense of ritual and chant. He could have been destined for
the priesthood, had not his overt homosexuality ruled out
that possibility. His music is sensual and atmospheric, using
harmony as colour in the French 'spectral' style and draw-
ing on the sounds of temple bells he discovered on travels
in Bali. At the age of thirty-four, Vivier was murdered by a
rent boy he had met earlier the same evening. Could he have
had a premonition? The score he was working on, entitled
Do You Believe in the Immortality of the Soul?, was a dram-
atised monologue about a journey on the metro in which
the narrator is attracted to a young man. The music breaks
off at the line: 'Then he removed a dagger from his jacket
and stabbed me through the heart.' Vivier's life ended the
same way. He called *Lonely Child*, in which a voice weaves
ethereally around bells, gong and vibraphone, 'a long song
of solitude'. At the time of his death, he had begun a vain
search for his birth mother.

'Nana' (Lullaby) (1914)

This tiny lullaby, 'Nana', is spare and to the point: sleep child, sleep; sleep my soul, go to sleep little star of the morning. Combining the simplicity of Andalusian folk music and the tender sophistication of Western art song, it is one of the *Seven Popular Songs* (*Siete canciones populares españolas*) Manuel de Falla wrote at the end of seven years in Paris, shortly before returning home to Spain in 1914 at the outbreak of the First World War. He dedicated it to Ida Godebska, who hosted evenings for artists and musicians in Paris and was a great friend of Ravel, in whose circle Falla moved. In 'Nana', an oriental mood makes the harmonies indistinct and mysterious, but the idiom is Spanish splashed with Arabic, the composer embracing his musical roots once more after a time of self-imposed cultural exile. With the words *Duérmete, niño, duerme*, a mother – or father – urges slumber and sees in the child hope for tomorrow: the morning star.

Since each composer had a childhood and started with an opus 1, formative works and pieces about early life are plentiful. It's not hard to find magnificent examples of 'official' first works: Schubert's song 'Der Erlkönig', Paganini's 24 Caprices, Fauré's *Cantique de Jean Racine*, Mahler's *Das klagende Lied* (later revised). Chopin wrote his first polonaise at the age of seven. Korngold composed his Piano Trio No. 1, a lush, romantic work full of dissonance, when he was a mere thirteen years of age. Webern's early *Im Sommerwind* belongs to a late-nineteenth-century Vienna on the brink of change. Piano works invoking childhood became popular post-Bizet, with Fauré's *Dolly Suite* and Debussy's *Children's Corner* leading the pack. Bartók's *Mikrokosmos* – 153 progressive piano pieces in six volumes – is one for every pianist, young or old, at least up to a certain point of difficulty. Mussorgsky's *The Nursery* songs, to his own texts, reflect his dark and fertile imagination. Kurtág's playful *Játékok*, Sofia Gubaidulina's *Musical Toys* and, in contrast, Schnittke's blowsy, exuberant score for *Clowns und Kinder* (1976) are among more recent offerings. You may not have come across Vítězslava Kaprálová (1915–1940). This young Czech composer's brief career began with Five Compositions for Piano, Op. 1. She's worth discovering. Elgar's *Wand of Youth* and his very late *Nursery Suite*, written for the young princesses Elizabeth and Margaret, show an older man looking back. Saint-Saëns's *Carnival of the Animals* has wit for young and old (though I have to say I find it maddening). Britten's *A Charm of Lullabies* abides by its description, and he wrote many works for the young – especially *A Ceremony of Carols* – but, for gleeful innocence, nothing beats his *Simple Symphony*.

2

LAND, SEA AND SKY

The fields were dazzling, fixed with frost,
and the crown of sunrise rose scarlet and crimson.

Sir Gawain and the Green Knight, translated by
SIMON ARMITAGE

Violin Concerto in E flat major, 'La tempesta di mare' ('Storm at Sea') (1725)

Rallying hunts, thunderous storms, flocks of twittering birds: these are the hallmarks of *The Four Seasons*, which has been popular since the rebirth of interest in Vivaldi's music in the 1930s after two centuries of neglect. The stormy cascades of notes, the mix of certainty and surprise, extend to his many other concertos. One that stands out is 'La tempesta di mare', the aptly named Violin Concerto in E flat major (RV 253). The brisk opening, with solo violin leaping across strings and the accompanying ensemble gusting and shuddering beneath, nearly blasts the listener away. Scales fly up and down like clothes tossed on a washing line in a high wind. Vivaldi (1678–1741) spent most of his life in Venice, a maritime-mercantile city then teetering on the edge of its last golden age of power, an island state built on a salt marsh, sheltered by the deceptively sleepy lagoon yet living on borrowed time. Vivaldi, eccentric priest and virtuoso violinist, spent half a century living at sea level, teaching homeless girls at the Ospedale della Pietà on the Riva degli Schiavoni, overlooking the waters of the Grand Canal. He died, impoverished, not in Venice but Vienna. His death was caused by 'internal fire', a brilliant description of how his music inhabits the soul long after the last note has sounded, but in fact probably a reference to bronchitis or pneumonia.

Overture: *Zaïs* (1748)

Rameau's pastoral fairy-tale opera, taken from Middle Eastern myth and stirred up with a dash of freemasonry, opens with shock and alarm, a solitary, muffled kettledrum and jerky, stop–start eruptions: the Earth's elements are distilled from primordial chaos (half a century before Haydn attempted something similar in *The Creation*, after peering through a telescope in Slough). In the subsequent prologue, Oromazès, king of the spirits, creates the world. After that the narrative is less secure, with a genie sacrificing all for love, a temple collapsing, and the lovers finding themselves alone in the desert. The Rameau Project, a joint venture between the Orchestra of the Age of Enlightenment and Oxford University, will complete work undertaken by Saint-Saëns who, together with Debussy and Vincent d'Indy, edited Rameau's music in the nineteenth century. A recent recording suggests that the overture really is the best bit. One witness in Rameau's day noted: 'I consider that the overture paints so well the unravelling of Chaos that it is unpleasant; this clash of Elements separating and recombining cannot have made a very agreeable concert for the ear. Happily, man was not there to hear it. The Creator spared him such an overture, which would have burst his eardrums.' Needless to say, audiences found this radical musical invention too disturbing and it was replaced with something more gentle for further performances.

RICHARD WAGNER

Overture: *Der fliegende Holländer* (*The Flying Dutchman*) (1843)

The opening of Wagner's overture to *Der fliegende Holländer* (*The Flying Dutchman*) flings us into the tempestuous world of German Romanticism with wind-whipped sea and plunging waves, evoked by lurching horns and furious blasts of screeching strings. Phantom Norwegian sailors steer a ghost vessel with blood-red sails and black masts, condemned to wander the high seas until the Dutchman finds redemption through the love of a good woman. The main musical themes of the opera, itself quite short, occur in this overture, which in contrast is quite long. Our concern in this instance, however, is not the synopsis, nor the complex background to the work's composition (a pleasure for another time) but the way Wagner conjures tempest, hurricane and raw fear of the wild in his orchestral writing. Wagner wrote in his memoir *Mein Leben* (*My Life*) that a rough sea journey from Riga to London in 1839 had set his mind whirring, the roar of the crew's shouts echoing round a Norwegian fjord feeding his musical imagination. In a sense this epic has a single protagonist: the sea.

ROUGH SEA, EASTBOURNE

CLAUDE DEBUSSY

La Mer (1905)

In photographs, Debussy always has the air of an elegant landlubber. Yet he once remarked, 'You're unaware, maybe, that I was intended for the noble career of a sailor and have only deviated from that path thanks to the quirks of fate. Even so I've retained a sincere devotion to the sea.' Debussy was working on his symphonic work La Mer – 'To which you'll reply that the Atlantic doesn't exactly wash the foothills of Burgundy . . .! And that the result could be one of those hack landscapes done in the studio.' It turned out that Debussy had plenty of chance to see the sea for real: he had fallen in love with the singer Emma Bardac, and travelled with her to Dieppe (seaside resort) and Jersey (island). Emma was pregnant with their child, Chouchou. His wife Lilly tried to commit suicide. In July 1905, Debussy escaped his terrible domestic drama and took a suite at the Grand Hotel, East-bourne, home of palm court and tea dance, where he would finish La Mer. 'It's a charming, peaceful spot,' he wrote. 'The sea unfurls itself with an utterly British correctness. In the foreground is a well-groomed lawn on which little chips off important, imperialist blocks are rushing around.' The music, glittering miraculously in a constant recreation of spray, salt sea and surge, is awe-inspiring and majestic. Debussy forgets that the polite waters of the English Channel lap happily at the shores of northern France. He might, were he alive today, prefer to use the tunnel.

'Bredon Hill' (1912)

A shy Etonian with a passion for Morris dancing, George Butterworth enlisted at the outbreak of the First World War in August 1914, twice being awarded the Military Cross for bravery. In this masterly setting of a poem from A. E. Housman's *A Shropshire Lad*, the cycle of seasons – of life, death, renewal – is compressed into a few short minutes. It opens with a joyous pealing of bells, chiming up and down the piano: summer on Bredon Hill in Worcestershire. The poet and his lover lie there together on a Sunday morning, hearing the skylark and looking down at the Cotswolds landscape. The mood shifts to wintry misery – a solitary lover, mourners at church – but still the noisy bells ring out again in hope. The song's mix of joy and melancholy feels all the more intense given Butterworth's own brief career. He died during the Battle of the Somme, in August 1916, aged thirty-one.

GUSTAV HOLST

Egdon Heath (1928)

Egdon Heath's stark moorland existed only in Thomas
Hardy's imagination, a brooding presence in his novel *The
Return of the Native*: 'A place perfectly accordant with man's
nature – neither ghastly, hateful, nor ugly; neither common-
place, unmeaning, nor tame; but, like man, slighted and
enduring; and withal singularly colossal and mysterious in
its swarthy monotony!' Holst used these words to preface his
fifteen-minute orchestral tone poem, an austere but radical
work that expresses a pagan spirit of place. While Holst was
working on the piece, he and Hardy had walked in rural Dor-
set, in south-west England, the region Hardy had brought
so potently to fictional life. Holst considered *Egdon Heath* his
greatest achievement. Vaughan Williams agreed, praising
'the bleak grandeur of its outline'. They were in a minority.
The premiere in New York took place on 12 February 1928,
just weeks after Hardy's death. Instead of celebrating this
new orchestral work, the event took on a lugubrious memorial atmosphere. A Danish actor read the opening of *The Return
of the Native*, according to a reviewer, in an 'audibly fitful' way.
The UK premiere the next day, which Holst conducted in
Cheltenham, was well received, even though the critic of the
Musical News and Herald sniffily remarked that *Egdon Heath*
'illustrates the sentimental reaction' of large-town composers visiting the country. Not much of a crime. Since most of
us now live in towns, Holst's music offers a welcome fantasy
exposure to the wilds, from the safety of an urban postcode.

JEAN SIBELIUS

Tapiola (1926)

Forests where the sun never reaches and the snow never melts: this is the landscape Sibelius conjures in *Tapiola*, his last and most magnificent orchestral tone poem, which left him anxious, depressed and reaching for the whisky bottle. His publishers, Breitkopf und Härtel, demanded hurried delivery of the manuscript before Sibelius was ready. He asked for cuts; they refused as the score was already engraved. Before the first performance in New York, on Boxing Day in 1926, the conductor Walter Damrosch gave a short introduction to the audience in which he described the infinite dark green forests where 'we hear the howling winds, whose icy sounds seem to come from the North Pole itself'. The music, inhabiting a world of Finnish gods and folklore, is like a single huge boulder, seen from near and far, in massive outline and in forensic detail, hewn from one thematic idea. Vast, noisy brass eruptions, shivering tremolando strings and ghostly woodwind evoke the forlorn vistas Sibelius loved. The music sounds slow-moving and glacial, yet the score is fast, mostly marked *allegro*. His explanation of the work, written in prose but turned into verse by his publishers and printed in the score, sums it up:

> *Wide-spread they stand, the Northland's dusky forests,*
> *Ancient, mysterious, brooding savage dreams;*
> *Within them dwells the Forest's mighty God,*
> *And wood-sprites in the gloom weave magic secrets.*

'Ritual Dances' from *The Midsummer Marriage* (1955)

The seasons, the cycle of birth, death and rebirth, the rituals of water and fire are key elements in Frazer's *The Golden Bough*, a late-Victorian study of magic and religion, which caused uproar by linking the traditions of Christianity with the tropes of pagan gods. It caught a mood and inspired T. S. Eliot, D. H. Lawrence, Naomi Mitchinson and W. B. Yeats, as well as Michael Tippett. The composer (1905–1998) explored life, literature, Jungian psychology, arcane myth and folklore with a restless appetite and a singular musical voice. Currently still eclipsed by his near-contemporary Benjamin Britten, and with old prejudices that he was too full of psychological fads and flakiness continuing to prevail, Tippett's time will surely come. The four dances from his *Magic Flute*-like opera, *The Midsummer Marriage*, have a soaring vitality hard to resist. The first dance depicts the earth in autumn, with the hound chasing the hare. In the second, opening darkly with clarinets – the water in winter – the otter chases the fish. Then comes spring; the hawk chases the bird. Listen for growling pizzicato strings, and bassoons. The fourth dance is about summer fire, the bonfires of St John's Night – Midsummer's Eve – and voluntary human sacrifice. The sudden injection of choral voices provides a blistering climax before all vanishes into silence.

OLIVIER MESSIAEN

Des canyons aux étoiles (1974)

An elemental horn call, then the rush of wind, the roar of the desert. This gargantuan twelve-movement work, 'From the Canyons to the Stars', celebrates the lonely grandeur of Bryce Canyon, its colours, sights and sounds, witnessed by Olivier Messiaen (1908–1992) and his musician wife Yvonne Loriod when they visited Utah in 1972. The work was commissioned by the great patron Alice Tully to celebrate the bicentenary of the American Declaration of Independence, and premiered in New York in 1974. In it we encounter all Messiaen's musical preoccupations, from Hindu rhythms to birdsong, synaesthesia and spirituality. The music journeys from the canyon to the stars and beyond to the celestial city itself. 'It is also a geological and astronomical work,' Messiaen said. 'The sound-colours include all the hues of the rainbow . . . the blue of Steller's Jay and the red of Bryce Canyon. The majority of the birds are from Utah and the Hawaiian islands. Heaven is symbolised by Zion Park and the star Aldebaran.' The state of Utah was so delighted with the piece that it renamed one of its peaks Mount Messiaen. For a more melodic, Technicolor depiction of this landscape, there's little to beat Ferde Grofé's popular *Grand Canyon Suite* (1931), piped through the sound system in the diorama of the Disneyland Railroad, full of distant thunder, crickets chirping and the open trail ahead.

HARRISON BIRTWISTLE

Silbury Air (1977, rev. 2003)

Silbury Hill near Avebury in Wiltshire rises up out of flat, grassy ground, smooth-edged, evenly shaped, flat-topped, almost featureless, like a steamed pudding turned from a giant's Neolithic cooking bowl. It is thought to be the largest man-made mound in Europe, mainly of chalk, added to and growing bigger in time, and comparable in date and size to the pyramids of Egypt. A road runs near, but the landscape is open, quiet. Its purpose is unknown, but the place has an earthy, arcane power, majestically expressed in this chamber piece by Harrison Birtwistle (b. 1934), a Lancastrian who has spent much of his adult life in Wiltshire. As the composer has said, 'Seen from a distance the hill presents itself as an artificial but organic intruder on the landscape.' In this fifteen-minute work, Birtwistle repeats and juxtaposes 'static blocks' of notes, according to a strict logic he has been unwilling to reveal. In his own terminology he has created an artificial sound landscape that reflects the hidden structure of the mound. Delicate, almost desiccated in the way the musical lines rise singly, without merging, *Silbury Air* sounds both sensuous and raw, new and immemorial. The end is abrupt, with plucked chords on that most unearthly of instruments, which happens to be the composer's favourite: the harp.

PETER SCULTHORPE

Kakadu (1988)

This buoyant symphonic work, complete with optional didgeridoo, conjures up the national park of Kakadu in northern Australia, an ancient wilderness of rugged mountain plateaux and coastal tidal plains. Peter Sculthorpe (1929–2014), who enjoyed a long career and influenced a generation of composers, was a pioneer in expressing Australia's landscape and culture in music, seeing his homeland not as an extension of Europe but as inextricably linked to South-East Asia. The music of *Kakadu*, he said, was suggested by the colours and rhythms of indigenous chant. 'Sadly, today,' Sculthorpe wrote, 'there are only a few remaining speakers of kakadu or gagadju. The work, then, is concerned with my feelings about this place, its landscape, its change of seasons, its dry season and its wet, its cycle of life and death.' It opens noisily and energetically, reaches a lull with a beautiful cor anglais solo, and unfurls into what might be imagined a sunset busy with bird life. Sculthorpe enjoyed his private tribute to another composer: 'Kakadu' is also the German word for cockatoo, used by Beethoven in his variations for piano trio inspired by 'Ich bin der Schneider Kakadu' ('I am Kakadu the tailor'), a comic song of the period. Nothing could be more remote from the monsoons and trade winds of northern Australia.

Three masterpieces of the great outdoors should be in everyone's library: Beethoven's 'Pastoral' Symphony, which has the best rain and the most malevolent thunderstorm; Richard Strauss's *An Alpine Symphony*, a grandiloquent representation of an epic, mountain landscape, and Britten's Four Sea Interludes from *Peter Grimes*, potent in the opera's drama but which stand alone, sparkling, spraying, roaring. For landscapes of snow and ice try Vaughan Williams's *Sinfonia Antartica*, which grew out of his film score for *Scott of the Antarctic* in 1947. Fifty years later Peter Maxwell Davies travelled to the South Pole and wrote a symphony (No. 8). 'The ice crashing along the bows was one of the most exhilarating sounds I ever heard,' he wrote. Rautavaara's *Cantus Arcticus* (1972) instead derives from the Arctic. Albéniz's *Iberia*; Borodin's *In the Steppes of Central Asia*, Mussorgsky's *Night on the Bare Mountain* are all musically and pictorially vivid. You could make a fairly full map of Britain from the works it has ignited: Mendelssohn's *Hebrides Overture* and 'Scottish' Symphony; Peter Maxwell Davies's *Start Point* and *Farewell to Stromness*, Harrison Birtwistle's *Grimethorpe Aria*, Vaughan Williams's *Norfolk Rhapsody*, Gurney's *Gloucestershire Rhapsody*, Holst's *Cotswold Symphony*, Bax's *Tintagel*. There's Elgar and the Malvern hills, E. J. Moeran in Norfolk and Ireland, Britten in East Anglia and South-East Asia. Further afield, explore the landscapes of Bohemia with Dvořák (not forgetting his New World travels) and Smetana; Austria with Bruckner and Mahler; India through the ears of John Cage, Messiaen, Philip Glass; America with Charles Ives, Steve Reich and John Adams. The list is endless. Bartók's *Out of Doors* and Copland's *An Outdoor Overture* have simple titles that speak for themselves.

3

ALIVE, OVERFLOWING

Happiness. It comes on
unexpectedly. And goes beyond, really,
any early morning talk about it.

RAYMOND CARVER, 'Happiness'

Crystal Palace. The Handel Orchestra

GEORGE FRIDERIC HANDEL

The Arrival of the Queen of Sheba (1748)

Two slender stelae, funerary monuments to kings and queens
of a lost empire, rise up from the ancient ruins of Aksum in
northern Ethiopia like huge stone telegraph poles. In the
1930s, Italian soldiers looted one and took it in massive pieces back to Rome. After decades of international negotiations
and logistical nightmares – each block capable of sinking the
wrong ship – in 2008 the obelisk arrived back home, greet-
ed by tens of thousands of joyful Ethiopians. Not quite the
arrival of the Queen of Sheba, since the monuments post-
date her, but this elusive royal figure – most 'facts' about
her are completely mythical – has long been associated with
Aksum, her story central to its founding myths. Seemingly
ubiquitous, Sheba appears in the Hebrew Bible, the Muslim
Koran, Turkish and Persian miniatures, Italian renaissance
art, Kabbalistic treatises and works of Christian mysticism.
Above all she is immortalised by Handel in some of the most
exuberant music he, or anyone, ever wrote: the short sinfonia for bustling strings and two prominent oboes from
his oratorio *Solomon*. For me, since early childhood, it has
symbolised exhilaration. My parents had it on an EP with
Handel's coronation anthem for George II, *Zadok the Priest*,
equally thrilling, on the flip side. I wore it out. That was
when you could wear records out. With the revival of vinyl,
the habit may start all over again.

JOHANN SEBASTIAN BACH

Singet dem Herrn ein neues Lied (BWV 225) (1724)

With one joyous explosion after another, each dazzling and bright as a sequence of detonating fireworks, this double- choir motet launches as it means to go on: 'Sing to the Lord a new song,' the psalmist demands, and 'sing, sing, sing' rings out from different voices in effervescent, uplifting harmony and darting, virtuosic counterpoint. The texts are from Psalms 149 and 150, and invoke praise through dance, through timbrel, through harp. Bach wrote the motet as part of the Lutheran liturgy for New Year's Day 1724, his first at the Thomaskirche, Leipzig. Years later, in 1789, it left an indelible impression on Mozart. He heard it in Bach's church and was overwhelmed. According to a witness: 'Hardly had the choir sung a few bars when Mozart sat up startled; a few measures more and he called out: "What is this?" ... As it finished he cried out, full of joy, "Now *there* is something one can learn from!"' The conductor John Eliot Gardiner has described the final section, 'Lobet den Herrn in seinen Taten', as sounding as though, with voices alone, Bach had 'dragooned all the Temple instruments of the Old Testament – the harps, psalteries and cymbals – into the service of praising the Lord, like some latter-day cuadro flamenco or big-band leader'. Bring it on.

Serenade in B flat major for wind ensemble ('Gran Partita') (1781)

'Extraordinary! On the page it looked nothing. The beginning simple, almost comic. Just a pulse – bassoons and basset horns – like a rusty squeezebox. Then suddenly – high above it – an oboe, a single note, hanging there unwavering, till a clarinet took over and sweetened it into a phrase of such delight! This was no composition by a performing monkey! This was a music I'd never heard. Filled with such longing, such unfulfillable longing, it had me trembling. It seemed to me that I was hearing the voice of God.' Antonio Salieri's words on encountering the *Adagio* from Mozart's extraordinary Serenade for thirteen wind instruments, nicknamed 'Gran Partita', sum up this music for us all. How better to describe such effervescent yet expressive music? Except that Salieri, maligned and lampooned by history as Mozart's small-minded rival, said no such thing. The words are imagined in Peter Shaffer's 1979 play *Amadeus*. Fictional or not, the older composer's realisation that he was in the presence of a genius has its own ineluctable truth. Nearly an hour long and in seven movements, the *Gran Partita* seeps into the brain with imperceptible force. The *Adagio* is the heart of the piece, the jubilant wit of the outer movements making the whole work all the more urgent.

LUDWIG VAN BEETHOVEN

Symphony No. 8 in F major (1812)

Asked why his Eighth Symphony was less popular than his Seventh, Beethoven gave a typically audacious reply: 'Because the Eighth is so much better.' He referred to it as 'my little symphony in F' and considered it his favourite. Together with his First, Second and Fourth Symphonies, the Eighth is still overshadowed in public perception by its towering siblings. It is compact, sunny, lithe and full of jokes (as in the tick-tock rectitude of the second movement, possibly a reference to the newly invented metronome). It may seem an unlikely chat-up ploy but I have proof. As a young man working in an office, my father whistled the opening bars (I suspect whistling-while-you-work is now banned). From across the room, not whistled but hummed, my mother – the pair had hardly met – offered the responding phrase. It clinched things. Soon they were married. So in a singular way you might say my brother and I owe our lives to Beethoven. Those opening phrases were a theme tune of childhood. Only later when I heard the work performed in full by a symphony orchestra, rather than in part by a whistler and a hummer, did I realise the two anticipatory notes my father always added at the start were his, not Beethoven's. It was one of those bewildering discoveries of growing up.

FRANZ SCHUBERT

Piano Quintet in A major ('Trout') (1819)

The title of Schubert's 'Trout' Quintet, a work overflowing with nonchalance and brio, relates as a set of variations in the fourth movement to a song the composer had written earlier: a capricious trout, a babbling brook, a cold-blooded fisherman, a twitch on his rod and a brutal end. Schubert completed the quintet in 1819 when he was twenty-two. It was played only once in his lifetime. The deliciously wriggly piano part adds to the work's buoyancy. It was the first chamber music I heard played live (taken aback to find that a little song could somehow grow into an enormous enterprise lasting forty minutes). Christopher Nupen's TV documentary *The Trout* (1969) has been a powerful advocate both of Schubert and of this quintet. Nupen captured on film the young Itzhak Perlman (violin), Pinchas Zukerman (viola), Jacqueline du Pré (cello), Zubin Mehta (double bass) and Daniel Barenboim (piano) rehearsing and performing the work. Their sense of fun, as well as their youthful musicianship, remain forever fresh. How many millions have been converted to classical music by that film? Cello and piano have many shared moments: Barenboim and Du Pré, not long married, made sparks fly. Soon Du Pré was suffering the first signs of the multiple sclerosis that ended her career. Many years later, I was lucky to work with Nupen, as much a perfectionist as the musicians he has immortalised on film.

JOHANNES BRAHMS

String Quintet No. 2 in G major (1890)

The giddying cello theme that opens this quintet prompts all the more pleasure because its source was such an unlikely personality. Brahms's music usually evokes darker moods. The man himself, though generous, and blessed with loyal friends such as Robert and Clara Schumann, was generally boorish, grumpy, a misfit who never found real love or solace. 'He who can create all this must be in a happy frame of mind,' observed his musical confidante Elisabeth von Herzogenberg, one of those European *cosmopolites*, shadowy yet popping up everywhere. Brahms wrote his Second String Quintet in G major, for two violins, two violas and cello, in the summer of 1890 in his favourite retreat at Bad Ischl, high up in the Austrian alps – 'Vienna by the Lakes' – where, in July 1914, Emperor Franz Joseph would sign the declaration that triggered the First World War. Sending the score to his publisher, Brahms gloomily wrote: 'With this note you take leave of my music because it is now high time to stop.' At fifty-seven he was ready to give up. Instead, this rampant work, with its generous double viola textures and dance rhythms, heralded an artistic Indian summer. Brahms's close friend Theodor Billroth, a pioneering surgeon and early student of music psychology, was at the first performance in Vienna in November 1890. 'I have often reflected on the subject of what happiness is for humanity,' he wrote. 'Well today, listening to your music was happiness.' It is.

SAMUEL COLERIDGE-TAYLOR

Ballade in A minor, for orchestra (1898)

Growing up in a mixed-race family in Edwardian Croydon, then a leafy town ten miles south of London, Samuel Coleridge-Taylor (1875–1912) was blessed unexpectedly, his talents encouraged. By six he was skilled at the violin and sang in the church choir. He won a place at the Royal College of Music and had supportive teachers. The Ballade in A minor was written for the 1899 Three Choirs Festival when Elgar himself was too busy to fulfil the commission. 'I wish, wish, wish you would ask Coleridge-Taylor to do it. He still wants recognition and is far away the cleverest fellow going amongst the young men,' Elgar pleaded. Coleridge-Taylor was just twenty-two. The result is catchy, exuberant and striding, so melodic it refuses to leave your head after only one hearing. Amid a blaze of publicity, the London press attended the performance in Gloucester. The critics were enthusiastic but had no idea how to discuss the music, using terms that now make us shudder: a 'peculiar blending of barbaric and Western modes', wrote one, while another praised its 'barbaric gaiety'. The *Musical News* thought Mr Taylor would 'tone down in course of time'. Luckily he did not. *Hiawatha's Wedding Feast* was about to explode on to an unsuspecting public, making its composer an international star.

Serenade for Strings (1892)

Elgar has ridden his bicycle around the different corners of this book before settling here. The Serenade for Strings Op. 20 might seem an unusual choice; compact, yet ardent and perfect. The Second Symphony, *The Dream of Gerontius*, the Violin Concerto, Violin Sonata, String Quartet, Piano Quintet – all jostled for a place. In the end the Serenade made the cut. This short piece converted me to Elgar after I played it on a summer music course as a teenager. It still instantly conjures the smell of cut grass. The first performance was given by the Worcester Ladies' Orchestral Class, which Elgar conducted. In that late Victorian era, even more socially divisive than anything we witness today, a violin craze was tearing through the educated classes – for women especially – just as brass bands were a compelling pastime for working men in the north. Elgar wrote music for both. No doubt these Worcester women, those who had to go out to work, were destined to play in cinema, restaurant or department-store bands if they were lucky. How inspiring to have the dapper, soigné composer introduce them to this new work: two irresistibly charming outer movements and a central section of prolonged rhapsody, with plenty of scope for hefty vibrato.

Sinfonietta (1926)

'The taxi radio was tuned to a classical FM broadcast. Janáček's Sinfonietta – probably not the ideal music to hear in a taxi caught in traffic.' So opens Haruki Murakami's cult 2009 bestseller *1Q84*, which goes on to explain, accurately, that the 'little symphony' was written as a fanfare for a Czech gymnastics festival in 1926. In the novel the year is 1985. Aomame is seated in a hushed Toyota Crown Royal Saloon on the gridlocked elevated Metropolitan Expressway in Tokyo, wondering what Janáček would have thought to know that his piece was being heard in such circumstances. She wonders, too, how, although no classical fan, the moment she heard the opening bars, 'all her knowledge of the piece came to her by reflex, like a flock of birds swooping through an open window'. Written late in Janáček's life, the Sinfonietta requires a big orchestra full of swaggering brass – three kinds of trumpets, plus horns, trombones, euphoniums, tubas – and has a glinting energy from the outset. It was 'written with a hot pen', Janáček said. Let Murakami, contemplating the reconfiguration of Eastern Europe, have the last word: 'This may be the most important proposition revealed by history: "At the time, no one knew what was coming." Listening to Janáček's music, Aomame imagined the carefree winds sweeping across the plains of Bohemia and thought about the vicissitudes of history.'

GIOACHINO ROSSINI

'La Danza' (1835)

The whirlwind lunacy of this Neapolitan patter song – 'Now the moon is over the ocean; Mamma mia, we're going to leap!' – encapsulates Rossini at his wittiest. The eighth song of *Soirées musicales* (1830–35), it is usually performed alone. Starting with a headlong gallop on the piano (there is also an orchestral version, sometimes a little turgid in comparison), the voice must keep up with the fleet-footed tarantella pace, jumping and whooping throughout, faster, faster, round and round until the next breathless leap. Liszt, Chopin and Respighi all produced their own versions: one reason the tune may sound familiar. From Enrico Caruso to Luciano Pavarotti, Roberto Alagna to Rolando Villazón, all have recorded it. One of the fastest and finest is by Joyce DiDonato, with Antonio Pappano as pianist. Taste the adrenalin. Hopping, jumping, turning, spinning. La la ra la ra, la ra la la ra la . . .

Clapping Music (1972)

In Steve Reich's *Clapping Music* only two pairs of hands make the rhythm, the melody, the harmony, the dance. As you listen, you can believe that music requires nothing but the percussive sound of one flat palm of one hand slapped against one flat palm of another. Spanish flamenco, Javanese gamelan and American gospel have always used clapping. Steve Reich wanted to compose a piece that 'would need no instruments at all beyond the human body'. It is in strict canon, achieved by one performer remaining fixed, 'repeating the same basic pattern throughout, while the second moves abruptly, after a number of repeats, from unison to one beat ahead, and so on, until he is back in unison with the first performer'. This idea of repeated patterns which shift gradually out of sync is key to Reich's work. *Music for Pieces of Wood* is one of many examples. Try out his *Clapping Music* app and hone your own rhythmic skills, following in the wake of, at time of writing, 40,000 others. Reich has said that even after performing the piece for more than forty years, he still gets nervous. If you prefer something with more harmony, go back four centuries to the exuberant verse anthem of Orlando Gibbons, 'O clap your hands'. It starts with the same idea.

Even the saddest music makes you feel alive, but the emphasis here was on cheer. Each of Bach's six *Brandenburg Concertos* fits the bill. So does so much Handel – the Coronation anthems, the *St Cecilia Ode* or *Dixit Dominus* – and Haydn – obviously *The Creation* but also witty works such as the 'Joke' String Quartet or the 'Surprise' Symphony. After long dithering, Beethoven's effervescent Symphony No. 1 yielded to his own favourite, the Eighth. Mozart's Piano Concerto No. 21 in C major (K. 467) was a contender on the simple basis that so perfect a work brings joy. Friends came up with ideas: 'You can't live without Chabrier's *España*, Grieg's *Wedding Day at Troldhaugen* or Massenet's Suite from *Le Cid*,' said one (in fact I can, but he can't). Tchaikovsky's *Souvenir de Florence* insisted another, to which I would add Hugo Wolf's *Italian Serenade* and Mendelssohn's 'Italian' Symphony. The 'Shrovetide Fair' opening of Stravinsky's *Petrushka* teems with life but the trajectory is dark. From a related sound world, his short *Scherzo à la russe* is an alternative. Dvořák's *Carnival Overture* and Leonard Bernstein's Overture to *Candide* are irrepressible. In quite different moods, so too are Smetana's *Má Vlast* and the *Polovtsian Dances* from Borodin's *Prince Igor*. Nancarrow's zany Study for Player Piano No. 21, which ends with one hand slowing down, the other speeding up, has to make you laugh. Steve Reich's upbeat, in every sense, *Music for 18 Musicians* is a great blaster of the blues. The *Hymn to the Sun* from Philip Glass's *Akhnaten* has appropriate radiance. For a solid five minutes of uplift, try Parry's anthem 'I Was Glad'.

4

CHANGE

*For know a better, fresher, busier sphere – a wide,
untried domain awaits, demands you.*

WALT WHITMAN, 'Song of the Exposition'

Veni Sancte Spiritus (early 14th century)

In his lifetime he was celebrated all over Europe, a musician of enormous influence but also a mathematician and astronomer. Few today know anything about John Dunstable (*c.* 1390–1453), or Dunstaple. He might have come from Bedfordshire, certainly travelled to Burgundy, definitely enjoyed aristocratic patronage, and conclusively was buried within the square mile of the City of London, at the church of St Stephen Walbrook. The rest is a blur. After his death, his music continued to be copied out – a sign of his reputation – and was listed in the great collection known as the Eton Choir Book. In an era of works by 'Anon.', and with the carefree late-medieval habit of recycling manuscripts, whether written over or cut up to use as bindings, a surprising 52 works by Dunstable survive. Why was he important? He was the leading exponent of a sweet, new and sonorous English style – the *contenance angloise*, so pure and direct in comparison to the complexities of some of his European colleagues, flowing in line, the text clear, the harmonies boldly consonant (using thirds and sixths, to our ear 'major'). The motet for Pentecost, *Veni Sancte Spiritus* ('Come, Holy Spirit'), for four unaccompanied voices, has precisely those qualities. Dunstable was a close contemporary of Brunelleschi, architect of the dome in Florence Cathedral. Perhaps this mysterious, polymath Englishman, whose own work heralded a new musical age, and the pioneering Italian Renaissance artist might once have met.

JOHANN SEBASTIAN BACH

Fantasia and Fugue in G minor (BWV 542) (before 1720)

Could this be the work, of all on this list, I would save – or which might in some sense save me – from earthquake, wind and fire? It has to be a contender. From that thunderous opening, a crash of dissonant trills and chromatic ornaments scatters forth as if hurled in fury from the great hands of Zeus himself. This mighty organ work travels incalculable musical and emotional distances. After that initial fortissimo cry, the music shifts in confutation to a mood of quiet reflection, steady and in four parts, before setting off again with new Herculean vigour. Now another gentle intermezzo follows before the *Fantasia* unfurls to a raging climax and a sudden bright chord ending. The *Fugue* grows from acorn to oak, speaking more directly than the intricacies and complexity of any technical analysis could hope to express. As so often with Bach, the exact circumstances of its writing are a question of debate and perhaps not of much interest: was he in Weimar or Cöthen? Was it a job application or a commission? With Bach the music outshines any such prosaic alibi. Some would argue that this work, too, is the source of all Gothick horror music, but that's another story.

LUDWIG VAN BEETHOVEN

Piano Sonata in B flat major, 'Hammerklavier' (1817–18)

'I am writing a sonata now which is going to be my greatest,' Beethoven told the composer Carl Czerny, his friend, piano-pedagogue and one-time pupil. The work would become the 'Grosse Sonate für das Hammerklavier'. With blunt wit, as well as understated accuracy given the extreme finger-wrestling, Beethoven told his publisher that the sonata would 'give pianists something to do', and that it would still be played fifty years hence. He wrote the sonata at the turn of 1817–18 after an unusual lull in his output: he had been ill with fever and had problems with a rude and irksome servant. The 'Hammerklavier' shocked Beethoven's circle. It still sounds wild. The music hurtles through unrelated keys, trampling over tradition like a riderless horse through undergrowth. There's humour too. The long *Adagio* is ethereal and profound. The final *Fugue* boils and spits, on the edge of incoherence. Beethoven's *Missa solemnis*, Ninth Symphony and *Diabelli Variations* – each a towering master-piece – were yet to come. As Alfred Brendel has written, 'We pianists are fortunate to have the chance to follow the path of his thirty-two piano sonatas . . . Who else offers the range from comedy to tragedy, from the lightness of many of his variation works to the forces of nature that he not only unleashed but held in check? And which master managed, as Beethoven did in his late music, to weld together present, past and future, the sublime and the profane?'

JEAN SIBELIUS

Symphony No. 3 in C major (1907)

'I am now in my prime and on the threshold of big things, but the years could easily melt away with nothing to show for them, unless I am taken in hand – above all, by me,' Sibelius wrote to a friend early in 1907. His drinking had gone too far. Debts were mounting. Full of ideas, he was also aware of his own frailty when it came to settling down to work. Things did not go entirely to plan: he was late with his Third Symphony, dithering over the finale all that summer. Yet out of the struggle, as if shedding old skins, a new style was born: lean, freewheeling, muscular and agile – music emerging from swirling mists. He called the last movement 'the crystallisation of ideas from chaos'. The whole work is intense and rigorous, at times peculiar, flowing and tumbling over strange, repeated patterns, with a surging outpouring of violas in the last movement. Sibelius composed barely a note after the Seventh Symphony, yet lived another three decades. The choice of the Third, over his Fourth (a particular favourite of composers), Fifth (rightly popular), Sixth (wonderful if neglected) or Seventh (one-movement genius), caused much hand-wringing. I have chosen the child most often overlooked.

ARNOLD SCHOENBERG

String Quartet No. 2 (1909)

In the course of its four movements, one world order is
shattered and a new one born. Schoenberg composed his
Second String Quartet at a time of personal crisis. Soon
after completing it he found out that his wife Mathilde had
been having an affair with their close friend and neighbour,
the young artist Richard Gerstl. When Mathilde ended it,
Gerstl hanged himself. The first performance, in December
1909, took place weeks after his death. Whether from hope-
lessness or hopefulness, Schoenberg dedicated the quartet
to his wife. From a relatively tender, tonal start – that same
twilight world of late Romanticism of his *Verklärte Nacht* –
the quartet gradually crosses into a new atonal universe, in
the last movement using all twelve notes of the chromatic
scale. More radically still, halfway through a soprano suddenly joins in. If, like those first audiences in Vienna ('brutish
and bestial', as Schoenberg called them) who wolf-whistled
and laughed and shouted, you find this hard on a recording,
try to hear it in concert. Then the mawkish 'wrong-note' use
of the nursery rhyme 'Ach du liebe Augustin', the tortured,
animalistic cry of 'Liebe' (love) in the third movement and
the sense of respite in the ethereal, urgent but radiant finale,
make sense. The second of two poems by Stefan George,
sung by the soprano, opens with the pivotal line: 'Ich fühle
Luft von anderem Planeten' ('I feel air from another planet').
So too did music history.

IGOR STRAVINSKY

The Rite of Spring (1913)

Like Uluru or Mont Blanc or Vesuvius or Popocatépetl, Stravinsky's ballet *Le sacre du printemps*, written for Diaghilev's Ballets Russes and the dancer–choreographer Vaslav Nijinsky, stands vast and immovable in the landscape. Whatever your vantage point, there's no escape – and nor should there be. With many rivals to choose from, the *Rite* remains the defining composition of the twentieth century. Stravinsky, agreeing that the two-part work had no clear narrative, said he had 'the vision of a great pagan celebration: wise old men sitting in a circle and watching the death dance of a young girl who is sacrificed to appease the god of spring'. The history of that first, riotous performance in Paris on 29 May 1913, the revolutionary musical techniques Stravinsky uses, the wildly radical orchestration, the reinvention – from that high, drunken, miaowing opening bassoon solo – of old Russian folk music for the modern age, the raw, elemental and orgiastic colours of the score itself: all has been told in hundreds of books and millions of words (worth, at the very least, a glance since the story can scarcely be done justice to here). Familiar even via Disney, who used it brilliantly in *Fantasia*, and a core work in the orchestral repertoire, *The Rite of Spring* still retains its power – primal, unearthly and, even on a hundredth hearing, cataclysmic.

Symphony in E minor (1933)

Racial prejudice, single motherhood, an abusive marriage and two divorces did nothing to deter Florence Price (1887–1953). If anything, these obstacles spurred her on. She made history. Born of mixed race in Little Rock, Arkansas, Price composed more than 300 works, many still unpublished. She gave her first concert aged four, and instead of following an expected career as church organist and music teacher set out to become a composer. After racial lynchings in Little Rock, Price moved with her young family to Chicago. It was the Depression. Her marriage ended. She played a cinema organ at silent movies to pay for food. Forced to take time off work in her mid-forties because of a broken leg, she wrote her Symphony in E minor. It was premiered by the Chicago Symphony Orchestra in June 1933, the first symphonic work by an African American woman to be played by an international ensemble. George Gershwin was in the audience at the 4,000-seat Auditorium Theatre. Adlai Stevenson flew in from Washington DC. President Roosevelt sent a note of congratulations: 'It comes at a time when the world needs nothing so much as a better mutual understanding of the peoples of the earth.' For a short time it seemed that Price might overcome discrimination. But back in Arkansas she attended a concert of her own music only to find a notice in the hall reading 'seats reserved for whites'. Her music, a mix of European, Southern and African American styles, is finding new support. Expect to hear more.

JOHN CAGE

Sonatas and Interludes (1946–8)

Screws, bolts, strips of rubber band, pellets of plastic insert-
ed between the steel strings with or without a screwdriver:
these are the unromantic ingredients, together with about
three hours, needed to turn a standard piano into a clank-
ing percussion ensemble. 'I placed objects on the strings,
deciding their position according to the sound that resulted.
So, it was as though I was walking along the beach finding shells that I liked, rather than looking at the ones that
didn't interest me,' John Cage said, describing his 'prepared
piano'. He wanted his Sonatas and Interludes, twenty short
pieces in all, to express the permanent emotions of Indian
aesthetics: heroism, eroticism, wonder, mirth, sorrow, fear,
anger, odium. Musicologists speak in terms of the work's
microstructures and ambiguous harmonies, its binaries and
its symmetries. It is better simply to listen. One pianist
(David Greilsammer) recently recorded some of the Sonatas
and Interludes interspersed with examples of the short, brilliant sonatas by Scarlatti: a vibrant way of inviting musical
pollination across two centuries, and an alternative way in.
Lasting around an hour and moving towards tranquillity,
the Sonatas and Interludes are among Cage's most influential early works, a new journey in sound and a step towards
the music of chance.

HENRYK GÓRECKI

Totus Tuus (1987)

This short choral outburst by the Polish composer Henryk Górecki (1933–2010) was written while Eastern Europe was in flux. It was first performed in Victory Square, Warsaw, in July 1987 in the presence of Pope John Paul II, whose motto was *Totus Tuus* (Totally Yours). Despite being ostracised by the authorities, Górecki had remained a Catholic during the Cold War years, riskily writing a piece for an earlier papal pilgrimage in 1979, when John Paul II first kissed the soil of his Polish homeland. That symbolic gesture helped ignite the Solidarity movement, triggering a series of events that would lead to the collapse of communism and the end of the Iron Curtain across Europe.

Górecki's own name became famous unexpectedly when his *Symphony of Sorrowful Songs* (1976) became an international bestseller in the early 1990s. The sudden celebrity knocked Górecki off balance. He finished his last complete work in 2004 and devoted time to his other love: wood carving, the traditional craft of the Kurpie forests of north-eastern Poland where he lived. His particular pleasure was to create something new from a single piece of wood. That wholeness is evident in the robust, joyful singularity of *Totus Tuus*.

Pli selon pli (1957–60)

Fold upon fold. *Pli selon pli.* Even translated, the meaning remains elliptical. The phrase comes from a sonnet by Mallarmé dedicated to the medieval city of Bruges. Boulez attempted an explanation: 'In the poem in question, the words "pli selon pli" are used by the poet to describe the way in which the mist, as it disperses, gradually reveals the architecture of the city of Bruges. In a similar manner, the development of the five pieces reveals, "fold upon fold", a portrait of Mallarmé himself.' Others have said that it is a self-portrait of the composer at a time of artistic crisis: self-questioning, struggling to comprehend the nature of creativity. The music, for large ensemble and soprano, is as intricate as the craft of lacemaking seen in the windows of the Belgian canal city which was, if indirectly, its inspiration. Pristine and alive, shimmering with the metallic colours of harp, gongs, celesta, tubular bells, it is startling in its emotional directness – not what we tend to expect of Boulez. Fold folding into fold. Version upon version. Between 1957 and 1960, *Pli selon pli* went through five different stages. Nearly thirty years later, the composer was still revising it. It ends with the word 'death', *'mort'*, and a massive, harrowing crescendo. If this were a history of music, Boulez's radical and influential *Le marteau sans maître* (1955) would have gone on this list instead. Choose either.

GABRIEL FAURÉ

'Les Berceaux' (1879)

Docks, quays and harbours have a special potency, the place where land meets sea, where journeys start and end. This poignant French chanson by Gabriel Fauré, with its rippling accompaniment, is at once a child's lullaby, a song of travel, a seafaring barcarole and a cry for home. Yet its essence is mankind's need to quest, to seek shining new horizons, and the pain such exploration causes, a theme as old as the *Odyssey* itself. Nothing in life is constant. The image of the women left on the quayside, or at home rocking cradles, while their menfolk sail the high seas, may be alien to us now – even if not everyone has the round-the-world yearnings of yachtswoman Ellen MacArthur. Either way the message and the conflict it embodies are universal. Fauré's *Mélodie*, by one of the most innovative and influential of songwriters, is poised, brilliantly controlled and wistful.

As with any art form, musical history is full of turning points. Bach's *Well-Tempered Clavier*, also known as *The 48 Preludes and Fugues*, which work through every major and minor key, transformed musical thinking, not least over the matter of tuning (that debate is still alive). Beethoven's Ninth broke the symphonic mould. Often a single work wins a reputation for bringing about a change that was already 'in the air'. Monteverdi's *Vespers* acted, in effect, as a bridge between Renaissance and Baroque. Wagner was credited with harmonic adventures that Liszt had already tried out in, say, his *Faust Symphony*. Leonard Bernstein called Berlioz's *Symphonie fantastique* the first musical exploration in psychedelia – fair enough – but its use of 90 instruments in the orchestra and its sheer aural invention, as well as its programmatic nature, were revolutionary. Tchaikovsky's *Pathétique*, by popular account a quasi-suicide note in music, was a vital work in other ways: the composer was pleased with his achievement, and the final slow movement was novel and influential – think of the slow ending of Mahler's Symphony No. 9. Many works reflect turning points in an individual composer's life: try Haydn's Symphony No. 22, Mozart's last three symphonies (Nos 39, 40, 41), Brahms's Symphony No. 4, Mahler's Symphony No. 1, Webern's Five Pieces for String Quartet, Op. 5, Schoenberg's Chamber Symphony No. 1, Varèse's *Ionisation*, Berio's *Sinfonia*, Shostakovich's Symphony No. 15, Terry Riley's *In C*, Gérard Grisey's *Partiels*, György Kurtág's *Officium breve*, Milton Babbitt's *Philomel*, Philip Glass's *Music with Changing Parts*, Cornelius Cardew's *The Great Learning*. A long list, but all ear-bending and mind-expanding.

5

LOVE, PASSION

'It looks easy enough. Let's try it.'

FLEUR ADCOCK, 'Coupling'

GUILLAUME DE MACHAUT

Quant en moy ('When Love Entered My Heart') (*c.* 1350)

The human chess game of medieval courtly love, played out between chivalrous knights and chaste maidens, might be dead, but traces indelibly remain. We can recognise that lover, depicted in this three-voice motet, so lacking in courage that he, now she too, is rendered petrified by fear of rejection. There is no mid-point between the hell of refusal and the heaven of acceptance for this poor suitor: 'I prefer to live in hope of mercy than to be slain by refusal.' Guillaume de Machaut (*c.* 1300–1377) was the most illustrious French poet and composer of the fourteenth century. His lyric verse influenced Chaucer and his music represented the peak of the 'ars nova' tradition. Born probably in the Champagne region near Rheims, Machaut wrote many secular motets, employing almost dangerous dissonance and restless wordplay, to our ears stark and unearthly. Think of the call of the corncrake. Each line sings a different text (in contrast to later motets where all sing the same words), two upper voices pulling together and apart over a simpler, drone-like lower voice. 'And I love too foolishly' – *folletement* – cries the lover, in a sour harmonic clash. Playing on the word 'amour', the tenor intones, 'Amare valde', meaning 'very bitter'. Very bitter indeed.

CLAUDIO MONTEVERDI

Lamento della ninfa (1638)

White with grief, the nymph weeps, staggering back and forth, stumbling through flowers in helpless despair. Bring him back, as he was before, she cries, the man I love, the traitor who has destroyed my life, or I might as well die. This is the burden of Monteverdi's *Lamento della ninfa* from his Eighth Book of Madrigals (1638), emotions that go straight to the heart of anyone torn apart by love. Scholars are divided over the work, some calling its excesses anomalous in Monteverdi's oeuvre, others identifying it as a short mad scene every bit as powerful as those found in nineteenth-century opera. It is certainly a potent oddity. Three male voices tell the sad story in squeezed, erotic dissonances which tighten like a mesh around the solo soprano – the lamenting nymph herself – in a mix of taunting vengeance and wretched sorrow. Throughout the six-minute piece, a repeated bass figure drags the harmonies insistently downward. The nymph, destroyed by that collision of fire and ice which is the lovers' lot, scatters her cries to heaven.

Sino alla morte ('Until Death'), Op. 7 No. 1 (mid-seventeenth century)

A virtuoso singer born out of wedlock in Venice, Barbara Strozzi (1619–1677) was also a prolific composer, possessed of wit, spirit and beauty. Her fiery cantata for high voice and continuo has one message: 'My love will never die.' More precisely, this particular lover, regardless of absence of jealousy, will cling on until death, and here are the tugging vocal laments, sighs and note-flurrying torrents to prove it. Only now is the full extent of Strozzi's output – including an extensive body of cantatas and other vocal works – being brought to the concert hall. Her mother was probably a young servant girl in the household of the noble poet Giulio Strozzi, a man of letters who, given his generosity to her, is likely to have been her father. As well as providing moral support, he welcomed Barbara into the academy of intellectuals that he ran. She studied with the great Venetian composer Cavalli and set many texts by her putative father. Even so, she did not escape the satirists, who pilloried her for her beauty and implied that she earned her living as a courtesan.

FRANZ LISZT

Petrarch Sonnets (1839–46)

Three Romantic piano pieces, each a meditation on love: that moment of realisation; the agitation of obsession; the memory of rapture. Liszt, a twenty-one-year-old virtuoso pianist, had fallen for the Countess Marie d'Agoult, an independent-minded, unhappily married mother of two daughters and six years Liszt's senior. Their elopement caused scandal. She lost custody of her children. She also, as the years progressed, lost sense of herself as she subsumed her own talents, as writer and historian, to become Liszt's muse. Theirs was one of the great love affairs of nineteenth-century intellectual Europe, lasting a decade and producing three daughters (one of whom, Cosima, would marry Wagner). Their travels through Switzerland and Italy resulted in an outpouring of piano music, gathered in the three books of *Années de pèlerinage*. The Italian Renaissance poet, Petrarch, wrote his sequence of poems to Laura, the idealised married woman he loved – if indeed she existed. The three sonnets chosen by Liszt – Nos 47, 104 and 123 – were first composed as song settings and form part of the second book of *Années*, the Italian years. As Marie d'Agoult's doubts and self-retributions grew, so too did her lover's fame and self-worth. Liszt and the countess never married. Hurt by his infidelities, she told him crisply that she would be his mistress 'but not one of his mistresses'. That was the end of the affair.

RICHARD WAGNER

Prelude to *Tristan und Isolde* (1865)

Impassioned, crazed, restless, cumulative, explosive. The first, yearning notes of the prelude to Wagner's opera *Tristan und Isolde* – which, by the by, are considered a landmark in the history of harmony and accordingly have been widely praised and parodied – embody the ecstasies and agonies that lie ahead. When you hear singers in the prime of life, or indeed beyond, singing the title roles, it's easy to forget that this couple from medieval legend are young lovers. The knight Tristan and his Irish princess are probably still in their teens; elderly King Mark, whom Isolde is destined to marry, a mere thirtysomething. Before hearing a note I was drawn to *Tristan* via T. S. Eliot's *The Waste Land*, which quotes from Acts I and III, including 'mein irisch Kind' and the repeated 'Öd' und leer das Meer', meaning 'desolate and empty the sea'. (Eliot, who worked on the poem in a bus shelter by Margate Sands, was staring at the Thames Estuary, not the Celtic Sea – desolate yes, but rarely empty.) Audacious, if not reckless, Wagner read aloud his own text to the opera to a very particular ménage, including his wife Minna, his married muse Mathilde Wesendonck, and his future mistress and wife Cosima von Bülow, then inconveniently married to the man who would conduct the premiere of *Tristan und Isolde*. This music comes with the warning: highly flammable.

Alto Rhapsody (1869)

Brahms suffered many blows to his lonely heart, never finding redemption through love. His life-long devotion to Clara Schumann, several years his senior and married to the composer Robert Schumann, never came to fruition even after she was widowed. For a time, Brahms turned his attentions instead to Robert and Clara's daughter Julie, though not so that anyone would notice. News, in the summer of 1869, that Julie was to be married appears to have surprised him. Clara noted, 'Johannes is quite altered, he seldom comes to the house and speaks only in monosyllables when he does come . . . Did he really love her? But he has never thought of marrying, and Julie has never had any inclination towards him.' Typically, Brahms spoke his feelings in the only way he could: through music. He called the Alto Rhapsody, for alto, male chorus and orchestra, his 'bridal song'. Who but Brahms could have made a wedding gift in such autumnal hues? The melancholy text, from Goethe's 'Harzreise im Winter' ('Winter Journey in the Harz Mountains'), tells of a young man out of love with life. Its three parts conclude with a heavenly male chorus seeking consolation as a thirsty man yearns for water in the desert. 'It is long since I remember being so moved by a depth of pain in words and music,' Clara wrote, as if full realisation had just dawned. 'If only he would for once speak so tenderly.' He does, and now for ever, through the emotion of this Rhapsody.

PYOTR ILYICH TCHAIKOVSKY

Fantasy Overture: *Romeo and Juliet* (1880)

This stand-alone 'fantasy overture' offers some of the most exciting and rapturous of all love music. Tchaikovsky, always self-critical, had three attempts at completing it, with much intervention from his composer friend Mily Balakirev, who first came up with the idea for a tone poem based on Shakespeare's *Romeo and Juliet*. He fussed around Tchaikovsky, offering tips on structure, themes, key signatures and, no doubt, colour of ink. A lesser composer but a generous man full of gutsy and louche opinions, Balakirev's reaction on first playing through the score speaks more of his own proclivities. He told Tchaikovsky he imagined the composer 'lying naked in your bath' with the young Belgian soprano Artôt-Padilla, perhaps the only woman to whom the homosexual Tchaikovsky was ever attracted, 'washing your belly with hot lather from perfumed soap'. The work opens with louring bassoons and clarinets, building up to a warring confrontation between Montagues and Capulets and opening out into a soaring, voluptuous love theme, the climactic, sobbing French-horn figure tugging at the heart as it moves towards a fateful close. Prokofiev's *Romeo and Juliet* ballet deserves its own entry. Here, reluctantly, it will have to be an add-on, but a special and sizable one.

Violin Sonata in A major (1886)

This is the perfect marriage gift and a supreme example of one musician's gift to another. César Franck's Violin Sonata – written when he was sixty-three years old – was composed for his friend and compatriot Eugène Ysaÿe. The virtuoso Belgian violinist and composer was less than half Franck's age. Unable to attend Ysaÿe's wedding, Franck (1822–1890) sent the manuscript of this violin sonata to be opened at the reception. Luckily a pianist friend was present. Luckily, too, she had practised the challenging piano part, having been told the secret in advance. Ysaÿe spent, so the story goes, a few moments looking through the music, then the pair gave a performance to the guests. More than three decades after Franck's death, Ysaÿe still performed his friend's master-piece, a work in every sense amiable, big-hearted, dreamy and vehement. The rhapsodic opening moment is followed by an urgent, excitable second movement, a freely expressive third and an irrepressible rondo finale. It appears Franck had started the work decades earlier for Liszt's daughter Cosi-ma (later Mrs Wagner), a woman hardly short of a musical dedication or two. Violinists refer to the ever popular work as the 'Frank Sinatra', which doesn't entirely do it justice though, like Ol' Blue Eyes, it does have a radiant and natural singing quality.

LEOŠ JANÁČEK

String Quartet No. 1 ('The Kreutzer Sonata') (1923)

Endless twists and twines of passion, real and imagined, are entangled in Janáček's First String Quartet. It is named after Tolstoy's 1889 novella, in turn inspired by Beethoven's famous sonata for violin and piano, which bears the chance nickname (after a violinist who never played it, since he found it too difficult) 'Kreutzer'. Tolstoy's story explores marital jealousy, lust, sexual abstinence, possible adultery and a crime of passion. It was immediately censored, but copies circulated widely. Janáček had written a piano trio triggered by the subject years earlier, but no manuscript survives. Some of its themes surface in this quartet. 'I had in mind the pitiable woman who is maltreated, beaten and murdered,' Janáček wrote to Kamila Stösslová, a younger married woman for whom the septuagenarian married composer had developed an infatuation. In response, she seems to have kept her distance, indulging him fondly but not feeding his desires. The quartet, its loose, declamatory style far from the patterns of Austro-German sonata form, hurtles into life, a frenzy of vehemence and pathos. The ideas are so compressed the whole work feels liable to explode. Janáček's Second String Quartet, 'Intimate Letters', is a direct expression of his feelings for Kamila. Who knows her reaction to the elderly man's obsession, but the music she helped inspire is unforgettable.

'Veggio co' bei vostri occhi un dolce lume' (*Seven Sonnets of Michelangelo*) (1940)

The title means 'I see through your lovely eyes a sweet light'. Britten completed the *Seven Sonnets of Michelangelo* when he was in Amityville, New York, in 1940, his relationship with the tenor Peter Pears, for whom they were composed, now firmly established. The cycle has always been seen as a gift of love, from the composer to his beloved muse and help-mate. The sonnets, however, are as much about rejection and unsatisfied desire: here, in Sonnet XXX, the needy lover is like the moon, illumined only by the lover's sun, ever fearing darkness and abandonment, helpless without him. The mood is poignant and impassive, the voice full of wide, plaintive leaps, a sad resignation sounding in the repeated piano chords and languorous arpeggios.

This should have been easy. Music speaks to the heart, to those carrying the joys and wounds of passion. Were songs the chief concern you could fill several books, starting with Beethoven's *An die ferne Geliebte* ('To the Distant Beloved') and Schubert's early 'Gretchen am Spinnrade' with some six hundred still to go. Add those by Schumann, Brahms, Wolf, Debussy, Fauré, Poulenc, Hahn and all love is covered. Some music becomes romantic by association: Rachmaninoff's Second Piano Concerto may not have needed the help of *Brief Encounter*, but it is hard to eradicate those Celia Johnson–Trevor Howard embraces. Countless works are dedicated to loved ones, or inspired by them: Robert Schumann gave his song cycle *Myrthen* to his bride Clara as a wedding gift; Mahler dedicated, among other works, his Symphony No. 8 to his wife Alma. Chopin's early muse – notably for the Second Piano Concerto – was a young countess. (He apparently dedicated nothing to his more famous lover, George Sand.) Wagner's *Siegfried Idyll*, for his wife Cosima, stands apart from his other music in mood and intimacy.

Sometimes the words are more potent than their refracted impact: both Lassus and Palestrina set the text 'Osculetur me' – 'Let him kiss me' – from the Song of Songs. Other works are downright rampant: the *Bacchanale* in Saint-Saëns's *Samson et Dalila*, or the equivalent, more repressed expression in Ravel's *Daphnis et Chloé*; the orchestral *Dance of the Seven Veils* in Richard Strauss's *Salome*; the *Ritual Fire Dance* in Falla's *El amor brujo*; Scriabin's *Poem of Ecstasy*, Messiaen's *Turangalîla Symphony*, Stuppner's *Extasis*. Debussy's *L'après-midi d'un faune* is sensual. If you really want something steamy there's Schulhoff's *Sonata Erotica* which leaves little to the imagination.

6

PAUSE

And I shall have some peace there, for peace comes
  dropping slow,
Dropping from the veils of the morning to where the
  cricket sings . . .

<small>W. B. YEATS</small>, 'The Lake Isle of Innisfree'

HILDEGARD OF BINGEN

Columba aspexit (Twelfth century)

'The dove peered in through the lattice window.' With these vivid words the German medieval composer–nun – as well as mystic, doctor, writer, botanist, artist – celebrates God's mercy in a single, mellifluous line of chant. The Latin text is rich in symbolism: jewels, cedar of Lebanon, stones, spices, the wings of an eagle, a fountain of purest water and the dedication of a temple. The work probably dates from the 1150s or soon after. By then, Hildegard (1098–1179) had set up her own women's monastery near the banks of the Rhine, and she had been recognised by the pope, but certainly not everyone, as a seer and visionary. Fierce though she evidently was, Hildegard called herself a 'poor little woman', a virgin nun who stood 'in the unsullied purity of paradise'. Her seventy-seven surviving chants, adorned only by endlessly spiralling melody, put earthly life on hold, as if suspended in ecstatic contemplation. When I was writing a book about Hildegard, the composer Tarik O'Regan, at the start of his career, wrote a choral piece based on *Columba aspexit* for the girls' voices of the Hildegard Choir, Oxford. He dedicated it to my young daughters, who sang in it at the time. Their choir sweatshirts, navy with 'Hildegard' emblazoned in white, would appear in the laundry basket, reminding me I had chapters yet to write. In those years, Hildegard of Bingen cast a strange, bright web on our lives.

HENRY PURCELL

Fantazias and In Nomines (1680–3)

Henry Purcell was born into a family of musicians in 1659, a pivotal time in English history. It marked that moment of chaos between revolution and restoration. The 'Lord Protector' Oliver Cromwell had died the year before. King Charles II would return to claim the throne the following year, 1660. Both events, the wretched burial of one and the jubilant coronation of the other, took place in Westminster Abbey, a five-minute walk from the Purcell family's home (off Old Pye Street, which became one of Victorian London's worst slums, nicknamed Devil's Acre by Dickens).

Purcell's brief life, so close to the centre of such extreme events, was as contradictory as the times in which he lived. His music was radical and conservative, public and deeply private. Who knows why, as a young man, he wrote his fifteen Fantazias for the viols. The genre was outdated, the flamboyant new king disliked 'Fancys', as they were also called, preferring the dance music played by his Twenty-Four Violins. Purcell made no discernible efforts to have them published. In these tenebrous works, balm to the soul, he spins elaborate counterpoint from minimal forces. Lines are imitated, inverted, reversed. Purcell's genius is at its most effective in the daring five-part Fantazia on One Note: the fourth part plays a middle C, tolling insistently throughout: ideal, if a little repetitive for the novice viol player, as long as he or she can count . . .

LILI BOULANGER

Vieille prière bouddhique (1917)

This 'Old Buddhist Prayer' for chorus, soloist and orchestra is one of the last flowerings of a talent severed it its prime. In her few short years, Lili Boulanger devoted herself chiefly to her compositions and to the pursuit of peace. 'She was aware that her life would be brief, her time measured,' observed her sister Nadia Boulanger, the great French pedagogue, friend of Stravinsky, teacher of Copland, Bernstein, Messiaen, Pierre Boulez, Philip Glass and guru of countless more, who outlived her younger sibling by nearly six decades. Born in Paris in 1893, Lili died in 1918 aged twenty-four. Despite the ravages of Crohn's disease, she managed to win the coveted Prix de Rome, the first woman to take that honour. Her work – choral, orchestral, chamber – is distinctive, close to the world of Fauré and Debussy in its poetic, sensual nature. Her name has always been in my consciousness. While still at school, I took part in a masterclass at the Royal College of Music with Nadia Boulanger, then over eighty. Shrouded head to toe in black, her English almost incomprehensible, her commands peremptory, she came from another era. As she barked her instructions, according to the sol-fa system with which I was unfamiliar, pointing at the piano, I can say quite truthfully I had no idea what I was supposed to do. The memory still evokes terror. I have often thought about the burden of love and pain Nadia carried through life following the loss of her brilliant younger sister.

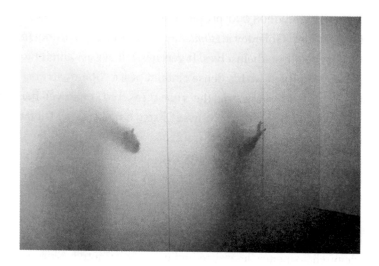

GYÖRGY LIGETI

Lontano (1967)

In 2007, some 208,000 people queued up to enter a glass box, Antony Gormley's *Blind Light*, in London's Hayward Gallery, and lose themselves. It was described as 'a luminous glass room filled with a dense cloud of mist. Upon entering the room-within-a-room, the visitor is disoriented by the visceral experience of the fully saturated air, in which visibility is limited to less than two feet. The very nature of one's sense of one's own body and its relationship in space to others is challenged.' Ligeti reached that point of mysterious, vaporous voyaging years earlier, in orchestral colour, in his 1967 one-movement work *Lontano* ('Distance'). Stretching, exhausting, excavating the possibilities of one line, one single pitch sequence, he created a fluid, contourless landscape of sound described by his biographer, Richard Steinitz, as 'a study in opalescence'. As listeners we can detect no metre, no rhythm or dynamic or accent, only a smooth flow of sound, which shifts slowly in and out of focus, layer upon layer of texture blending into one. Late on we sense a crisis, at once climactic and radiant, a high D sharp. Ligeti said: 'Suddenly there yawns an abyss, a huge distancing, a hole piercing through the music. It is a moment that has an irresistible association for me with the wonderful painting by Altdorfer, *The Battle of Alexander*, in which the clouds part and behind them is a beam of golden sunlight shining through.'

DMITRI SHOSTAKOVICH

24 Preludes and Fugues (1950–1)

Picture this, described by an eyewitness. In May 1951, an extraordinary event took place in the Small Hall of the Union of Composers. On two successive evenings, Shostakovich performed his most recent work, his 24 Preludes and Fugues for piano. While he was playing, he appeared oblivious to a tense situation unfolding all around him. When he finished, the chairman gave him the floor. As he addressed his colleagues, Dmitri Dmitrievich's face showed extreme exhaustion, as if he had just run a long-distance race, but at the same time a naïve credulity shone through his words: 'I wrote this work from October to February of this year. What was my aim? The first thing that stimulated me was my visit to the Bach celebrations in Leipzig.' Keenly anticipating the reaction of his colleagues, Shostakovich explained how he knew Rimsky-Korsakov had written sixty fugues as a training in polyphony, and that Tchaikovsky also wrote such a work. One by one, the Union secretaries and functionaries voiced their disapproval: 'This work is based on a grave miscalculation.' 'This music is ugly. I reject it categorically.' 'The composer expresses emotions that are morbid, gloomy and unhealthy.' 'This work does not correspond to the strict criteria of today's Soviet art.' And on, and on. Somehow the work has survived. Stop all the clocks. Lock yourself away. Listen.

Rothko Chapel (1971)

Morton Feldman was big and noisy. His music is so quiet you strain to hear it. At 30 minutes, *Rothko Chapel*, for soprano, alto, choir and small ensemble, is one of his shorter works. 'To a large degree my choice of instruments (in terms of forces used, balance and timbre) was affected by the space of the chapel as well as the paintings. I wanted the music . . . to permeate the whole octagonal shaped room.' Open to all as a place of meditation, the Rothko Chapel in Houston, Texas, is also a story of immigration: John and Dominique Ménil, the couple who commissioned it, escaped their French homeland in the Second World War. The abstract expressionist Mark Rothko, whose works hang on the chapel's walls, was born in Latvia. He arrived at Ellis Island in 1913 aged ten and grew up in Oregon speaking Russian, Hebrew and Yiddish. Feldman (1926–1987) was born in Queens, New York, the child of Russian Jews. Some of this autobiography is in *Rothko Chapel*. Feldman told the composer Gavin Bryars, 'The piece begins in a synagoguey type of way; a little rhetorical and declamatory. And as I get older the piece gets a little abstract, just like my own career . . . closer to the late pictures that are in the chapel in that kind of one hue of a colour . . .' A tune in the middle is a little Stravinsky-like. 'I wrote that tune the day Stravinsky died. So it was Stravinsky, Rothko, dead.'

'Pause' (*Die schöne Müllerin*) (1823)

'Pause' is from Schubert's cycle of twenty Lieder to poems by Wilhelm Müller that make up *Die schöne Müllerin*, about a young man who falls in love with a miller's daughter, believes for a moment that she returns his feelings, then sees his hopes dashed. This forlorn song is at the turning point of the cycle: in his blinkered optimism and ecstasy, the young man's heart is too full to sing. Here we see him not by the brook or the mill but in his own abode. He hangs his lute on the wall with a green ribbon and asks for rest, for quiet, waiting only until the wings of a bee or a whispered breath of air caress the strings to make music once more. Whether he wants a pause from turbulent emotions or from music itself is open to question. Paradoxically this is a song about *not* singing. The ribbon flutters across the strings of his lute until, quietly, they sound. Is this an echo of love's sweet anguish, or the hopeful first notes of a new song?

KARLHEINZ STOCKHAUSEN

Stimmung (1968)

'*Stimmung* will yet reduce even the howling wolves to silence,' Karlheinz Stockhausen wrote of his shimmering work for six amplified vocalists, who sing one note and its overtones for over an hour, arranged in a circle with the lights turned low. Shaped by his experiences as a hospital orderly in wartime Germany, Stockhausen embraced the artistic freedoms of the 1960s as a drowning man grabs rock. The Summer of Love was made for him. In April 1967 he was teaching at the University of California, Davis. His landscape was San Francisco Bay, the Golden Gate Bridge and the Pacific coast to Carmel. 'I used texts written in love-bitten times,' Stockhausen said. He ditched one wife and married a new one (the painter Mary Bauermeister) on a Sausalito houseboat while still involved with another lover. He completed the work that winter on Long Island Sound. 'I just watched the white snow on the water in front of my two windows. That was the only landscape I really saw during the composition of this piece.' He drew on the sounds of babies and lovers breathing, and the traditional singing techniques of Inuits, Tibetans, Tuvans. *Stimmung* was premiered in Paris in 1968 with the performers sitting cross-legged, in bare feet, wearing bright shirts or embroidered dresses. The title means 'tuning' – of the voice, a group of people, the soul. One critic, barely suppressing derision, called it 'a hippies' camp fire'. What should we gain from listening? 'Something of the unknown' was the essence of the composer's reply.

TORU TAKEMITSU

From me flows what you call Time (1990)

'My music is like a garden, and I am the gardener. Listening to my music can be compared with walking through a garden and experiencing the changes in light, pattern and texture.' Make that a Japanese garden, with its singular elements of water, rock, sand, gravel, an aesthetic of the miniature and the sculpted, of hide and reveal, of a meaningful space, or void. Toru Takemitsu (1930–1996), small, lean, gentle, had piercing eyes ready to smile and a serene air of melancholy (I interviewed him in his last years). Few composers physically match their music quite so precisely. As a soldier in the Second World War, Takemitsu absorbed Western culture. Eventually his friendship with the American John Cage, then steeped in Zen principles and 'roll of the dice' chance, turned him back towards his Japanese heritage. East and West meet fruitfully in *From me flows what you call Time.* The work was commissioned for the Boston Symphony Orchestra and its Japanese music director, Seiji Ozawa. At the premiere in 1990, five solo percussionists were linked to bells around the theatre by coloured ribbons representing water (blue), fire (red), earth (yellow), wind (green) and sky (white). The instruments conjure up ethereal, crystalline music: glockenspiel, marimba, vibraphone, steel drum, Pakistan Noah bells, crotales, Thai gongs, angklung, Arabic (or Turkish) drum, wind chimes, a set of boobam (or log drums), tom-toms, side drums, tam-tams, Chinese cymbals, Japanese temple bowls – a seemingly endless inventory of sound.

ARVO PÄRT

Tabula Rasa (1977)

Whether by melting wax or erasing chalk, the medieval notion of wiping the slate clean sings out in *Tabula Rasa*, for two violins, strings and prepared piano. It sounds deceptively simple. Music out of silence, music returning to silence, one movement with motion, one without; one speeding up, one slowing down. Arvo Pärt's first works, of the 1960s, were heavily criticised first for their serial techniques, then for their religious tendencies, neither acceptable to the authorities in Soviet-controlled Estonia. The composer retreated into his own artistic 'pause' in the early 1970s, writing almost nothing for eight years and converting to Russian Orthodoxy. During that time of crisis he laid aside atonality and explored early plainchant and Renaissance polyphony. In effect he scrubbed clean his musical palette and emerged with a new, sparsely notated style he called 'tintinnabuli', from the idea of bells pealing, in stillness and flux. The technique has exacting rules, but Pärt's own description is best: it is 'a space I sometimes wander into . . . where everything unimportant falls away'.

If there's one thing to make some of us tense it's the idea that listening to music is relaxing. I need to sit bolt upright to listen. When a friend told me that, to help her sleep, she listened to 'chanting monks' (a craze that began at least two decades ago at the dawn of 'New Age' music and has lasted), I realised we might have communication problems. The idea of 'pause' here is to find works that, whether in scale or structure or colour, demand a particular concentration that empties the mind of other concerns. The strong patterns of baroque music help and support our listening. Try the opening *Adagio* of Handel's Keyboard Suite No. 2 in F major for serene intensity. Satie's *Gymnopédies* or, in extremis, his *Vexations* – which in full performance takes about eighteen hours (who can blame the *New York Times* critic who fell asleep?) – offer that release for many. Mompou's *Musica callada* ('Silent Music') consists of twenty-eight short piano works, quietly expressive and not far, except in their brevity, from Morton Feldman's music, most of which could feature here. Luigi Nono makes an art of silence interrupted by notes in his quartet *Fragmente-Stille, an Diotima* (1980). La Monte Young's improvisatory *The Well-Tuned Piano* and Philip Glass's *Music in Twelve Parts* share a similar long-distance amplitude. Howard Skempton's *Lento* and Meredith Monk's *Songs of Ascension* still the mind. If you have only minutes to spare try Andrzej Panufnik's *Lullaby*, at once captivating and disturbing, or, a much loved encore, Sibelius's tender *Valse Triste*, though it does get rather jaunty at the end. Time to get on with life.

Zeppelin Wreck. East Anglia. June 17th. 1917.

7

WAR, RESISTANCE

One man to five, a million men to one.
And still they die. And still the war goes on.

JAMES FENTON, 'Cambodia'

GUILLAUME DUFAY

Missa L'homme armé (*c.* 1460)

The man, the man, the armed man. Fear him. Cry out everywhere. Arm yourself with your own coat of iron mail – your
haubregon de fer. These, in precis, are the words of a rustic
secular song, 'L'homme armé' ('The Armed Man'), thought
to have originated in Burgundy in the tenth century, at once
political and satirical. In the Middle Ages and Renaissance,
more than forty mass settings were based on this song. One
of the earliest was by the Franco-Flemish composer Guillaume Dufay (1397–1474). Born near Brussels, he travelled
to Italy and Savoy, an admired and highly influential figure,
and worked in the service of the Burgundian court. Among
countless theories (one is that 'L'homme armé' was a tavern)
is that by the fifteenth century the 'armed man' was identified with the last Valois duke, the warmongering Charles
the Bold of Burgundy. After Charles's death, bloodily in battle, the duchy of Burgundy collapsed, its lands divided, but
Dufay, too, was dead by then. Ockeghem, Palestrina and, in
our own times, Peter Maxwell Davies made versions, but
none has reached the popularity of *The Armed Man: A Mass
for Peace* (1999) by the Welsh composer Karl Jenkins. Dufay's
Mass, one of his most extensive works, is elaborate, complex
and graceful. If you want to unlock the riddles hidden in it,
you must steep yourself in the techniques of early Renaissance polyphony. There is no need.

JOSEPH HAYDN

Missa in Angustiis in D minor ('Mass in Troubled Times', 'Nelson' Mass) (1798)

Triggered by a warning call of trumpets and drums, Haydn's 'Nelson' Mass is one of his most glorious choral works. As with so many nicknames, this one was probably not of his making. The British routed the French at the Battle of the Nile in 1798, a victory that made Rear-Admiral Sir Horatio Nelson a hero, but Haydn completed the work before news reached Austria. In any event, Europe was already torn apart by years of French Revolutionary wars. Ever prodigious in output, Haydn lived his days in strict observance, rising early at 6.30 a.m., giving piano lessons before breakfast, working all day, consuming only a little bread and wine for supper and retiring at 11.30 p.m. Yet Haydn was exhausted in this period. The success of another choral masterpiece, *The Creation*, had left him spent. He was seen taking the sulphur baths at Schützen, near Eisenstadt in Austria, home of his long-time royal employers the Esterházy family. Too worn out to stray far from home, he wrote the new Mass in a matter of weeks. Since the prince had dismissed several wind players from the court orchestra – was he saving money, or were they incompetent? – Haydn made do with strings, trumpets, timpani, organ and bassoon. Rule-breaking, defiant and even joyful, with jubilant fugal choruses and a disturbing *Benedictus*, this is truly a work for uncertain times.

Etude in C minor, Op. 10 No. 12
('Revolutionary' Etude) (1831)

The opening chord crashes out like a warning shot, followed by a bombardment of fast notes from top to bottom of the keyboard and a tumultuous devil dance of right-hand heroic lament and left-hand furious attack. The instruction at the start of this short work is *con fuoco* – with fire. The young Chopin, barely in his twenties when he composed the 'Revolutionary' Etude, has compressed the anguish of a nation at war into a few minutes of virtuosic, impassioned piano music. Written in 1831 at the time of Poland's failed rebellion against imperial Russia, it has another name: 'Etude on the Bombardment of Warsaw'. The very heart had been torn out of Chopin's homeland. He was too sickly to fight, but spoke of the shock and pain of these events. The Etude is the last in his Op. 10 set, dedicated to 'my friend Franz Liszt'. This virtuosic work is a battle cry, a call to arms. Or, given the technical demands made on the pianist, a call to both arms. It was used, with other Chopin music, in the Tom and Jerry cartoon *Snowbody Loves Me*. (I think this is where I first heard it.)

MAURICE RAVEL

Le Tombeau de Couperin (1914–17)

Written out of deep friendship and affection, this is not obvious war music. Airborne and feather-light, the opening *Prélude* to these short works hides music of tenderness, hidden under a guise of formality. That was Ravel's style. In person he had a reputation for being sarcastic, aloof, impatient of *babillage* (prattling), obsessed with microscopic detail, unwilling or unable to show emotion. The *Tombeau* (with the same root as the English word 'tomb', meaning a musical work denoting a memorial) was Ravel's last set of piano pieces. It is a homage both to the baroque composer François Couperin, and to several of Ravel's friends who died in action in the First World War. (Ravel himself was keen to enlist but, too short, too old and suffering from a heart condition, he finally signed up as an artillery lorry driver.) Each movement is dedicated to one of the dead, with the exception of the *Rigaudon*, a tribute to two brothers killed by the same shell. The pianist Marguerite Long, widow of one of the dedicatees, gave the work's premiere in 1917. Later Ravel wrote his masterpiece, the Piano Concerto in G, for her (based on an idea that came to him on a train journey from Oxford to London). In response to a suggestion that the *Tombeau* should be more elegiac, Ravel said, 'The dead are sad enough in their eternal silence.'

OLIVIER MESSIAEN

Quatuor pour la fin du temps (*Quartet for the End of Time*) (1941)

January 1941. Temperatures below freezing. A German prisoner-of-war camp in Görlitz, Silesia. Four musicians, one of whom is a composer and organist, the Frenchman Olivier Messiaen. The others are a clarinettist, a violinist and a cellist. This was the unpromising circumstance that gave birth to the *Quatuor pour la fin du temps*, or *Quartet for the End of Time*. The audience for the premiere was a group of prisoners with their guards in the front row. One guard in particular had been supportive to Messiaen, providing him with materials and enabling him to work. 'Never have I been heard with as much attention and understanding,' Messiaen recalled later. The work is a meditation on words from the Book of Revelation, in which the Angel of the Apocalypse descends from heaven, 'clothed in a cloud, having a rainbow on his head' and declares: 'There will be no more Time: but on the day of the trumpet of the seventh angel, the mystery of God will be completed.' Four movements involve all the players, the lines variously flowing, throbbing, nervously jabbing and ethereally floating. At the heart of the work are two *Louanges* – hymns of praise – for solo cello and piano in the middle, and for violin and piano at the end. In life, music can exist only in earthly time. Messiaen was looking beyond.

Symphony No. 7 in C minor ('Leningrad')
(*c.* 1939–42)

In the winter of 1941–2, a quarter of a million people died in Leningrad, a city under siege by German and Finnish forces. As spring came, so corpses were revealed beneath the melting snow. Shostakovich had originally intended to dedicate his Symphony No. 7 to Lenin. Instead it became a tribute to the city that took his name. Only fifteen players could be found for the first rehearsal there in 1942, the work having been premiered in March that year, a thousand miles away in Kuibyshev. These few survivors were cold, starving, emaciated. 'Why don't you play?' the conductor Karl Eliasberg, himself skeletally thin, asked his solo trumpeter. 'I'm sorry, maestro, I haven't the strength in my lungs,' came the reply. Any soldier capable of playing an instrument – including some jazz musicians barely able to read music – was ordered to join the orchestra, persuaded by offers of extra food. Eliasberg cycled round the city searching for players. Shostakovich's enormous work, lasting one and a quarter hours, starts with a bright, unbowed string melody and a wistful flute solo before the battle, in all its grotesque fury, begins with a hushed, advancing snare drum. The conductor Semyon Bychkov, who was born in Leningrad and whose mother endured the 900-day siege, speaks of the work as 'a cry of the heart, against death and for life'.

BENJAMIN BRITTEN

War Requiem (1962)

Britten's emotionally charged statement about the pity of war was first performed on 30 May 1962 at the new Coventry Cathedral and broadcast live (nearly hazardously: the red sandstone building was hardly finished). The medieval edifice had been bombed by the Luftwaffe in the Second World War – in an operation, with terrible irony, code-named 'Moonlight Sonata' – leaving only its blackened shell, imaginatively left intact by the architect Basil Spence. Both reconstruction and music reflected the spirit of the late 1950s: tentative renewal, on the eve of the modern age. Coventry will forever carry an indelible association with Britten's work. Wrapped within the Christian litany, about which the composer had his own reservations, and the war poetry of Wilfred Owen, *War Requiem* uses huge forces. Massive brass fanfares, tolling bells, large chorus, boys' voices, soloists, plainchant, chamber organ and the colours of Balinese gamelan unite in contrast and certitude. A very early childhood memory is of my family going on a day trip to see the new Coventry Cathedral, immediately established as a cultural icon with its art by John Piper, Jacob Epstein and Graham Sutherland. Too young, I was left behind, abject. The place took on an elusive mystery. It was not until Britten's centenary year, 2012–13, that I eventually went to Coventry, for the unforgettable fiftieth-anniversary performance of *War Requiem* given by the City of Birmingham Symphony Orchestra, which had played at the premiere.

GEORGE CRUMB

Black Angels (1970)

Black angels, fallen angels, devils, near death, death itself. 'There were terrifying things in the air,' the American composer George Crumb (b. 1929) said of the Vietnam War years, when this work was written. Subtitled 'Thirteen Images from a Dark Land', this offers no easy aural embrace. It rewards close attention. Do not attempt to listen on your commute to work or while the children are shouting. Hear it live in concert first if you can. Written for amplified string quartet as well as a collection of water-tuned crystal glasses, metal thimbles and suspended tam-tam gongs played by the four instrumentalists, it is at once unsettling and moving. Crumb, a numerology obsessive, dated his score: 'Friday the Thirteenth, March 1970 (in tempore belli)' – in time of war. Sounds of insects' wings beating, the rattle of bones, a Dowlandesque lachrymae pavan based on Schubert's song 'Death and the Maiden', a dance of death, the tritone from Tartini's *Devil's Trill* and a *Dies irae* (day of wrath) all occur in this haunting exploration of good and evil, a modern masterpiece.

'Noël des enfants qui n'ont plus de maisons' (1915)

This little-known, bitter lament for refugees the world over was the last song Debussy wrote. Its mood is both popular and violent, its anger alas timeless. The composer was ill, and depressed by news of war. Set to his own text and dated 1915, it speaks of homeless French children at Christmas whose houses have been ransacked and destroyed by the enemy. Papa is away at war, Mama is dead, the school has been burnt and the schoolmaster too. The children have no toys, no wooden shoes and no bread. They pray for the little children of Poland, Serbia, Belgium and beg: 'Grant victory to the children of France.' Debussy died, aged fifty-five, in Paris in 1918. The city was under heavy bombardment, days after the start of the German Spring Offensive. The boulevards were deserted as the illustrious composer's body was carried to its rest.

Music, via fanfares and reveilles, was long used as a means of communication in war. An account of the Third Crusade describes a trumpet sounding on the battlefield in Syria in 1191. The Italian Renaissance historian Machiavelli, in his *The Art of War*, stated that the trumpet was an ideal noise to sound orders because of its piercing tone. Most works 'about' war are as much about the desire for peace, or a memorial to the dead. Vaughan Williams's poignant *A Pastoral Symphony* (1922) acts as an elegy to the Great War. John Foulds's epic *A World Requiem* (1919–21) is a great communal work, requiring 1,250 performers. Arthur Bliss's *Morning Heroes* (1930) for orchestra, narrator and chorus is similarly ambitious. Tippett, a pacifist, wrote his secular oratorio *A Child of Our Time* at the height of the Second World War. Schoenberg's *A Survivor from Warsaw*, Villa-Lobos's Symphony No. 3 (*A Guerra*) and Penderecki's *Threnody for the Victims of Hiroshima* explore the suffering of war. Britten's *Sinfonia da Requiem*, Nielsen's Symphony No. 4 ('The Inextinguishable') and Stravinsky's Symphony in Three Movements were written in wartime. The cinema has added to the canon: Prokofiev's *Alexander Nevsky*, Walton's *The First of the Few* and *Henry V*, Shostakovich's *Five Days, Five Nights* and *Volochayev Days*. Shostakovich's Symphony No. 8 is arguably an even darker contemplation on war than No. 7 ('Leningrad'). Barber's *Adagio* (1936), one of the few American works to be played in the Soviet Union during the Cold War years, has become a quiet anthem of peace. In our own time, Ligeti (Requiem), Peter Maxwell Davies (Naxos Quartet No. 3), Steve Reich (*Different Trains* and *WTC 9/11*), John Adams (*On the Transmigration of Souls* and *Doctor Atomic*), Simon Bainbridge (*Ad Ora Incerta*) and Colin Matthews (*No Man's Land*) have added tellingly to the genre.

8

JOURNEYS, EXILE

Many cities of men he saw and learned their minds,
many pains he suffered, heartsick on the open sea . . .

HOMER, *Odyssey*, Book 1, translated by
Robert Fagles

Three Latin Masses (1590s)

William Byrd's three Latin Masses, spare and often dissonant, are the work of a composer in exile in his own land.
Byrd (1543–1623) lived a double life. He wrote services for
the new Protestant liturgy, was favoured by Elizabeth I, and
was a Gentleman of the Chapel Royal. He was also a clan-
destine Roman Catholic, constantly at risk of persecution
and torture, his wife cited as a recusant. While Byrd's Great
Service, incorporating Matins, Eucharist and Evensong,
was written for large double choir and public performance at
the Chapel Royal, the three Latin Masses were designed for
small forces, to be sung in secret. By this time, no English
composer had set the Latin Mass publicly for thirty years.
They were published in the mid-1590s with Byrd's name on,
but with no named publisher or publication date. You can
see why. In 1581 the priest Edmund Campion was hanged,
drawn and quartered at Tyburn (near London's Marble
Arch). A young man who witnessed that death, Henry Walpole, wrote a poem bristling with treason entitled 'Why do I
use my paper, inke and penne?' Soon after, his publisher was
murdered as a traitor. Later, Byrd himself set Walpole's text
as a part-song for five voices and, a royal favourite, survived
unscathed. He omitted certain verses, including these chill-
ing lines: 'England look up, thy soil is stained with blood,
thou hast made martyrs, many of thine own.'

DOMENICO SCARLATTI

Keyboard Sonata in D major (K. 492/L. 14) (mid-eighteenth century)

'He goes, like a wayfarer, to meet every opportunity that may present itself for him to become known,' the Italian baroque composer Alessandro Scarlatti said of his traveller son Domenico (1685–1757). Seeing the world might have been only part of it. As with many a child of famous parents, Domenico wanted to escape his father's shadow, not least since they were in the same line of business. The feeling was mutual. Alessandro Scarlatti made several attempts to send the young man away from Naples, calling him 'an eagle whose wings are grown; he must not remain idle in the nest, and I must not hinder his flight'. Nor must he steal my lime-light, Papa Scarlatti might have added. Domenico worked in Venice and Rome but spent nearly thirty years in Portugal and Spain, absorbing Iberian musical styles into the outpouring of short, dazzling keyboard sonatas – some 555 in all. Little is known about which were written where, so it's a risk to call the music 'Spanish'. Still, some commentators enthusiastically speak of Scarlatti's fiery compositions, with their dissonances, avalanches of notes and zestful ornament, as imbued with Andalusian folk song and the click of castanets, as if the composer himself had on his flamenco gear. Yet listen to, say, K. 492 in D major, with its startling, abrupt rhythms and percussive ornaments, and it's hard to deny the presence of *duende*, that proud, untranslatable strut of haughty passion.

24 Preludes (1835–9)

Sometimes it seems as if longing for the homeland is a deeper emotional resource than actually being there. On 7 November 1837, Chopin set sail from Barcelona to Palma, Mallorca, in search of warmth to heal his frail body. He took little except new manuscript paper, some compositions in progress and his volumes of Bach. His companion was George Sand, his illicit, bisexual, cross-dressing lover – the idea was to escape scandal in Paris where she was, at the very least, a controversial figure, loathed or admired, with little between those two extremes. 'Here I am in Palma, among palms, cedars, cacti, olive trees, oranges, lemons, aloes, figs, pomegranates etc. . . .' wrote Chopin. Happy at first, within days he was ill: 'I've been as sick as a dog . . . All this is having a wretched effect on the Préludes . . . my manuscripts sleep while I get no sleep at all. I can only go on coughing and await the spring . . .' A further deterrent was the delayed arrival of a piano, which he relied on for the process of composition. Nonetheless, it was here in Mallorca that Chopin completed his revolutionary 24 Preludes, one in each key, following the example of Bach's *Well-Tempered Clavier*, which was a touchstone to him all his life. If 'prelude' in Bach's case meant being followed by a fugue, for Chopin it was a self-contained work that led only to another lustrous gem and then on to another. One of the longest, No. 17 in A flat, was Clara Schumann's favourite. Mine too.

Viola Sonata (1919)

Rebecca Clarke (1886–1979) was a pioneer, through inclination and force of circumstance, but often thwarted in her long life. She was one of the first female musicians to join the Queen's Hall Orchestra in London, as a viola player, in 1916 at the invitation of Sir Henry Wood (founder of the Proms). Clarke's life was full of contradictions: her father, displaying oppressive cruelty, both encouraged and later stalled her musical studies (was it her fault if her harmony teacher proposed marriage to her?). In part to escape family pressures she went abroad to work, later settling in New York. On one of these trips, in Hawaii in 1918–19, she wrote the Viola Sonata, which would become her most admired achievement. Clarke's career as a composer was intermittent. She came close to winning competitions but felt discouraged and accepted a position as a nanny. Late in life she married – she was nearly sixty – and the new stability helped persuade her back to music. The Viola Sonata, rich, expansive, late Romantic and soulful, remains her best-known work. She submitted it to a competition anonymously. From 72 entries it was initially voted joint winner. One critic thought it was by Ravel, another that 'Rebecca Clarke' was a pseudonym for Ernest Bloch, the eventual winner.

EDGARD VARÈSE

Amériques (1919–21, rev. 1927)

'As I worked in my Westside apartment . . . I could hear all the river sounds – the lonely foghorns, the shrill peremptory whistles – the whole wonderful river symphony, which moved me more than anything ever had before. Besides as a boy, the mere word "America" meant all discoveries, all adventures. It meant the unknown . . . new worlds on this planet, in outer space, and in the minds of man.' Born in Paris in 1883, living variously in Turin, Paris and Berlin, Varèse arrived in New York on 29 December 1915. He was newly divorced, had been invalided out of the First World War and had lost several of his manuscripts in a Berlin warehouse fire. America was a new start. He sought a new musical style. 'Musical organisations were run entirely by society ladies who certainly did not want to hear any modern music,' he wrote, soon after arriving. His first score in the new-found land was *Amériques*, opening with a melancholy solo flute and written for a vast line-up which included nine percussion players, ten trumpets, eight bassoons and three tubas. The sound of New York Fire Department sirens brings the world of the modern city into the concert hall. Sinister, exciting, barbaric.

GEORGE GERSHWIN

An American in Paris (1928)

Distracted by his long-running Broadway triumphs, Gershwin was raring to get back to orchestral music when he wrote *An American in Paris*. This is the brighter side of being away: abroad thoughts from home. Gershwin wrote the piece overlooking the Hudson River in New York. 'I love that river and I thought how often I had been homesick for a sight of it, and then the idea struck me – An American in Paris, homesickness, the blues.' After starting work on it, he decided to return to Europe for a quick refresher. Paris, in spring 1928, was one long party. He met the A-list wherever he went: Walton, Ibert, Poulenc, Prokofiev, Milhaud, Ravel, Diaghilev. He shopped long and hard to buy four authentic French taxi horns to recreate rush hour in the Place de la Concorde in his new piece. ('When I go this way with my head you go quack-quack-quack like that,' he instructed friends in a run-through in his hotel.) Mostly the music is cheerful and only faintly Gallic, with a debonair Broadway smile and a touch of inebriated fun, until a bluesy tune breathes a sigh of melancholy: 'intense and simple', before 'bubbling' back to life, as Gershwin put it. The work was first performed by the New York Philharmonic on 13 December 1928. One critic, Oscar Thompson, in a sneering verbal assassination, called it 'clever whoopee' – a wonderful phrase that, despite the writer's negative intentions, sums up the piece brilliantly.

Symphonic Dances (1940)

'Only one country is closed to me – and that is my own country, Russia.' The dark spirit of Rachmaninoff's words, in an interview given in 1930, tinges every note and bar of his final compositions. He had left revolution-torn Russia on an open sledge on Christmas Eve 1917, escaping first to Finland and then travelling to the US. During Rachmaninoff's quarter of a century in America – from 1918 until his death in 1943 – he wrote only six works. Did he spend too much time giving concerts and being a celebrated pianist? Or had he, as many have argued, left his soul in his homeland, almost silenced by loss? He sought out other exiled Russians – the pianist Vladimir Horowitz, the bass Feodor Chaliapin. He tried, too, to recreate the salon mood of Russia before the revolution, in his home in Beverly Hills. It was here that the composer and Horowitz played the two-piano version of Rachmaninoff's final work, the Symphonic Dances. Desperate to finish it for the start of the new concert season, during which he had commitments as a pianist, Rachmaninoff worked long hours until, as his wife recalled, 'his eyes refused to focus because of the work of writing the score in his small hand'. Waiting on railway stations while on tour, he used to pull the proofs from his suitcase and make final corrections to this work, which opens with sinister flares, darkens into a *valse triste* and ends with a macabre *Dies irae*. Rachmaninoff numbered this work among his favourites.

BÉLA BARTÓK

Concerto for Orchestra (1943)

Béla Bartók was fifty-nine when he sailed into New York
in 1940 to escape Nazi-occupied Hungary. Homesickness
never left him. Soon he told a friend, 'My career as a composer is over.' Quiet, slight, frail, Bartók imagined returning
to the tranquillity of home, away from the throng of Man-
hattan. He never did. He was already ill with leukaemia. He
gave concerts as a pianist, but no one was interested in his
own music. Two fellow Hungarian immigrants – the violinist Joseph Szigeti and the conductor Fritz Reiner – persuaded the great Russian conductor Serge Koussevitzky
to commission him. The Concerto for Orchestra was the
result. The opportunity to work again provided a temporary
cure. Bartók laboured on this glittering masterpiece at the
Adirondack Cottage sanatorium by Lake Saranac in upstate
New York. It was premiered by the Boston Symphony
Orchestra in 1944. The concerto starts in flickering darkness, with soft, shuddering low strings interrupted by a solitary flute melody. Snatches of European folk song, collected
by Bartók himself, entwine themselves round the brightness
of his New World music, ending in a bravura finale. Bartók
died in 1945 soon after obtaining American citizenship. His
funeral was attended by only ten people, mostly Hungar-
ians. In 1988, at the request of his sons, his remains were
returned to Budapest for burial, his exile finally ended.

FREDERIC RZEWSKI

Winnsboro Cotton Mill Blues (1980)

Real worlds collide in this ten-minute pianistic blast. Born in Massachusetts into an immigrant family and sharing a first name and nationality with Chopin, the American Frederic Rzewski (b. 1938) appeared destined from birth to become a pianist–composer. His elite education took him to Harvard and Princeton. He encountered the European avant-garde and might have settled for a concert career. Rzewski had other ideas. His best-known piece, *The People United Will Never Be Defeated,* is based on a Chilean protest song. This smaller *Blues* travels to the cotton mills of Winnsboro, South Carolina. Using every conceivable piano technique, Rzewski captures the oppressive noise – rollers, pickers, ginners; whirring and spinning – of the factory floor. All builds to chaos. Then a smoky blues melody curls up from the silence. Textile workers sang the original song in the General Strike of 1934:

> *Old man Sargent sitting at the desk,*
> *The damned old fool won't give us no rest.*
> *He'd take the nickels off a dead man's eyes,*
> *To buy a Coca-cola and a Pomo Pie.*

There really was a foreman called Homer Sargent. Tracked down by a journalist decades later, an old man in his nineties, he wasn't amused to find his managerial methods had sparked a song recorded by Pete Seeger and others, and this punchy masterpiece by a Polish-American with revolution in his heart.

'Heimweh II' ('Homesickness'), Op. 63
No. 8 (1874)

Brahms never suffered political persecution, nor did he travel extensively, but his music has a longing, a sense of exile from the happiness and love he sought all his life. He wrote three songs about homesickness or nostalgia, all by the minor poet Klaus Groth. This, the second, is the most gripping in its quiet anguish. The flowing piano part, gentle arpeggios, keeps the forward momentum, suddenly stopping abruptly on the bleak words 'In vain I search for happiness' before ending with a melancholy, comforting return to broken chords. 'Oh that I knew the way back', the poet reflects, to the safety of childhood, the tenderness of a mother's love, a retreat from this desolate, barren shore which we call life.

The sprawling notion here was the sense of being remote from that safe harbour, literal or psychological, we call 'home'. Many song cycles – from Schubert's *Winterreise* to Vaughan Williams's *Songs of Travel*, to Tippett's ('Sure, baby!') 1960s cultural extravaganza *Songs for Dov* – explore journeys. Countless works conjure place in relation to mankind, rather than (as in the *Land, Sea and Sky* section) nature and the wild. So Elgar's *In the South*, Liszt's *Années de pèlerinage*, Berlioz's *Harold in Italy*, Respighi's *Pines of Rome* and *Fountains of Rome*, Falla's *Nights in the Gardens of Spain* and Albéniz's *Rapsodia española* all belong here. Great cities are immortalised in countless works, even when the nickname came later: Mozart's 'Prague' Symphony, Haydn's 'London' Symphony, Vaughan Williams's *A London Symphony*, Delius's *Paris: The Song of a Great City*, Ives's *Central Park in the Dark*. Pauline Viardot's extensive travels led to songs about Madrid and Florence. Schumann's 'Rhenish' Symphony bears the river Rhine in its title, but every note sings of the great cathedral city of Cologne. In Heiner Goebbels's *In the Country of Last Things*, after Paul Auster's novel, the city is unnamed. The now unfashionable nineteenth century idea of 'orient' inspired Balakirev's *Islamey* and Rimsky-Korsakov's *Scheherazade*. Roussel's *Evocations* recalls travels in Indochina and to Angkor Wat. Milhaud's *L'Homme et son désir* grew out of his time in Brazil. Britten's study of gamelan while on holiday in Bali in 1956 surfaces in his ballet *The Prince of the Pagodas*. Giles Swayne's *CRY* followed time spent in the Gambia and Senegal. Luigi Nono's last composition, the fragmentary *'Hay que caminar' Soñando* for two violins, was prompted by graffiti he saw on a wall: 'Travellers, there are no paths, you have to walk.' The performers move between six music stands, literally seeking out the music: journey, exile and homecoming in one.

9

GRIEF, MELANCHOLY,
CONSOLATION

It is a stubble field, where a black rain is falling.
It is a brown tree that stands alone.

GEORG TRAKL, 'De Profundis', translated by
James Wright

JOHN DOWLAND

'Flow My Tears' (*Lachrymae*) (1604)

'Where night's black bird her sad infamy sings, There let me live forlorn,' lamented John Dowland (1563–1626) in his best-known lute song 'Flow My Tears'. Opening on a falling phrase, then with an upward gasp before falling again and again, the notes themselves drop in squeezed harmonies like tears of anguish. The song grew out of his instrumental collection, *Lachrymae, or Seaven Teares Figured in Seaven Passionate Pavans*, a study of weeping from sad tears to those of joy and gladness. These lute pavans give full leash to grief. Dowland was a shadowy figure, a spy and a papist who thought little of leaving his wife and three children behind in England to earn large sums abroad. Rose Tremain's novel *Music and Silence*, set in the Danish court of Christian IV where Dowland was a well-paid musician, depicts him tellingly: 'The man was all ambition and hatred, yet his ayres were as delicate as rain.' An obsession with melancholy had swept through Renaissance Europe, epitomised by Shakespeare's depressive Hamlet: 'But I have that within which passeth show; These but the trappings and the suits of woe.' Richard Burton's *Anatomy of Melancholy* (1621) gave the subject full, forensic study. A treatise by Timothy Bright warned of the risks of a poor diet, counselling against plovers, sparrows, sodden wheat, porpoise, eel and salt fish. For Dowland, the tears 'which Musick weeps' offer the greatest consolation.

Music for the Funeral of Queen Mary (1695)

All talk at the St Cecilia's Day feast of 1694, where a new *Te Deum* and *Jubilate* by Mr Henry Purcell was performed in the presence of King William and Queen Mary II, was of smallpox. The disease had already claimed 1,325 victims. The diarist John Evelyn noted, 'An extraordinarily sickly time especially of the smallpox, of which divers considerable persons died.' By 28 December the queen too was dead. The funeral, reckoned by Evelyn to have cost £100,000, eventually took place in early March 1695. The streets were draped in black cloth, with gravelled paths and black-wrapped handrails designed specially by Christopher Wren. John Blow and other composers had written tributes. It was music by Purcell, however, that probably accompanied the funeral cortège on its journey from Whitehall to Westminster Abbey. Four trombones ('flatt trumpets') played his 'March for the Queen's Funeral, Sounded Before Her Chariot'. A muffled drumbeat accompanied the procession (requiring 20 yards of black baize to cover five drum cases at a total cost of £3 10s, according to the Lord Chamberlain's accounts). Eight months later, on the eve of St Cecilia's Day, 21 November 1695, the 'English Orpheus' himself died. Purcell was thirty-six. Music he had written for the queen became his own funeral lament. His memorial in the north choir aisle of Westminster Abbey, where he had been organist, reads: 'Here lyes Henry Purcell Esq., who left this life, and is gone to that blessed place where only his harmony can be exceeded.'

Cantata 106: *Gottes Zeit ist die allerbeste Zeit* (*Actus Tragicus*) (*c.* 1707)

To recognise the shortness of life is to confront the fear of death. In these or similar words, many a philosopher or theologian has struggled to help mankind deal with mortality. With poignant serenity, this same thought tolls through Bach's early funeral cantata, the *Actus Tragicus*. The text expresses the realisation that we shall all die when our time – God's time – is right, and if we learn this and put our house in order we shall be wise. No one is certain whose death was being marked: perhaps an uncle, or the young wife of a close friend, both having died around the time the piece was written. Bach, orphaned early in life and still in his early twenties, conveys grief through simple means, with a twenty-bar 'sonatina' opening for two recorders, two violas da gamba and organ. The instruments throb a steady pulse throughout, while the recorders twist and wrap around each other, as if enfolding the melodic line in mutual sorrow. The effect is unadorned, the achievement complex and precisely balanced. With or without religious faith on the part of the listener, this music speaks to heart and soul.

HECTOR BERLIOZ

Tristia (1831–48)

'The composer of the Fantastic Symphony thoroughly looked the part,' wrote a youthful acolyte after meeting Hector Berlioz (1803–1869) towards the end of his life. So vivid is the young man's description, you might wish he had become a novelist instead of, as it turned out, a conservatory professor. Not always flattering, his words are rich in detail: 'A mane of grey, almost white, elegantly wavy hair, an eagle's beak of a nose, fine drawn, powerfully arched brows beneath which glittered two penetrating eyes, a tragic forehead, more broad than high, a thin-lipped mouth at once mocking and proud, a delicately sculpted chin, gave his face an expression of bravery and incomparable poetry . . . his voice with its strange timbre and abrupt, pungent delivery, the fire of his glance and his sparing but electrifying gestures . . . The glamour of this person magnetised my whole generation.'

Their conversation ranged round a 'torrential current' of topics that obsessed Berlioz: music, art, books, historical figures and, above all, Shakespeare and Berlioz's favourite play, *Hamlet*. Why have you not written an opera on *Hamlet*, the young man asked. Berlioz replied, 'I would never dare. I did compose three entr'actes for [*Hamlet*], which I called *Tristia* – "sad things". When I am consumed with melancholy I perform my music and listen to it within myself.' These three settings for orchestra and chorus were written at different times and published in 1852. Berlioz never heard *Tristia* performed in public.

ALBAN BERG

Violin Concerto (1935)

Berg's only solo concerto started out simply as a rather generous commission, in 1935, from the celebrated Ukrainian-American violinist Louis Krasner (1903–1995), who also teased compositions from Schoenberg, Alfredo Casella, Henry Cowell and Roger Sessions. Krasner was its dedicatee but another name, and a tragic story, has made the concerto famous. Berg was working on his opera *Lulu*, but broke off (it was never finished) to work on the new piece. In the course of writing it, Manon Gropius, the eighteen-year-old daughter of the Bauhaus architect Walter Gropius and Alma Werfel (Mahler's widow), died of polio. Berg had known her since her childhood. The loss traumatised him. He wrote to Alma saying the score would be dedicated 'To the memory of an angel'. The work starts with the four open notes of the violin, evolving into music of anguish and sorrow, via a twelve-note row, a Carinthian folk song and a statement of Bach's Lutheran chorale, 'Es ist genug' ('It is enough'). Whether you approach it as a defining example of twentieth-century music, in which serialism and tonality collide, or whether you prefer to dwell on the strange beauty of the sound, this concerto wears its grief openly. For Berg, as he told Alma, it summed up 'that which I feel and today cannot express'. Through his music Manon Gropius, and Berg's love, live on.

RICHARD STRAUSS

Metamorphosen (1945)

Kurt Vonnegut immortalised the phrase 'So it goes', using it 106 times in *Slaughterhouse-Five*, his novel about the fire-bombing of Dresden by Allied forces on 13 February 1945. He was in the Saxon city at the time, a twenty-three-year-old US soldier who survived the air raid by hiding in a meat locker. The novel wasn't published until 1969, at the height of the Vietnam War. In the introduction, Vonnegut wrote, 'There is nothing intelligent to say about a massacre.' Richard Strauss's response to the bombing, by contrast, was immediate. He was an old man, in despair at the ruin of all he had known: 'My beautiful Dresden – Weimar – Munich, all gone!' Within weeks the German composer, nine of whose operas had been premiered in Dresden, wrote *Metamorphosen* for twenty-three solo strings. Its dark opening, with a cello phrase climbing up from the gloom, only to be pulled back down by the quietly sobbing phrase of two violas, embodies lament. On a cold, wet Sunday afternoon a few years ago, two dozen string-playing colleagues – working in music, as writers, publishers, publicists, agents, but usually keeping our performances discreet – gathered to read through *Metamorphosen*, conducted by the versatile (and on this occasion foolhardy) broadcaster Tom Service, the twenty-fourth person. We managed it twice through, reasonably competently, and then, as I recall, made new friends and ate well-earned cake. Spirits were high. So it goes.

FRANCIS POULENC

Stabat Mater (1950)

In his idiosyncratic fashion, Francis Poulenc embraced the
Roman Catholicism of his youth after a visit in 1936 to the
shrine of the Black Virgin at Rocamadour in south-west-
ern France. He returned there often, 'putting under the
protection of the Black Virgin' various works, including
his *Stabat Mater*, dedicated to the memory of his friend, the
artist Christian Bérard (*see left*, 1902–1949). Known by the
pet name Bébé, Bérard designed Cocteau's ornate fantasy
film *La Belle et la Bête* (1946). He worked with Dior, Coco
Chanel and Nina Ricci, and lived a relatively open gay life
with Boris Kochno, a director and librettist associated with
Diaghilev's Ballets Russes. Their glittering circle included
Balanchine, Cole Porter and Szymanowski. This was Poulenc's world too: a life of love, sweet sentiment, unresolved
sensuality and religiosity, regret, melancholy, sorrow and,
above all, wit, however mordant it might be. All these elements, with opulent choral writing and the soprano rising
above, are present here, in a work Poulenc called 'a requiem
without despair'. 'The *Stabat* is going at such a speed,' he
said, after visiting the shrine in 1950, 'that it is certainly a
miracle of Rocamadour.'

GIACOMO PUCCINI

Crisantemi (1890)

This impetuous expression of grief, a single movement for string quartet, was written at top speed by an impassioned, youthful composer who from then on wrote almost nothing but opera. It might not be a masterpiece but Puccini's *Crisantemi* ('Chrysanthemums') has a touching directness. He wrote it in 1890 following the death of the popular Amedeo di Savoia, Duke of Aosta, second son of the Italian king, Vittorio Emanuele II. The two minor-key melodies on which the music centres reappear in Puccini's first great operatic success, *Manon Lescaut* (1892), as the lovers Manon and Des Grieux struggle across the empty wilderness of Louisiana towards their fate. The instruction in the string quartet is *Lento triste*: slow, sad. According to the composer's own recollection, he completed it 'in one night'. Since Amedeo died on 18 January and the piece was first performed, in Milan, eight days later on 26 January, he can hardly have been exaggerating. The applause was so enthusiastic at the premiere that the musicians, the Quartetto Campanari, immediately repeated the six-minute work. It was scarcely played again in Puccini's lifetime.

JONATHAN HARVEY

Mortuos Plango, Vivos Voco (1980)

If you cannot believe music made with tape and comput-
ers has heart or soul, this might convince you. Ancient and
modern, ethereal and timeless, this otherworldly piece was
mixed at IRCAM, the sound research institute set up by
Pierre Boulez as an extension of the Centre Georges Pom-
pidou in Paris. Jonathan Harvey (1939–2012) was himself
nervous: 'In entering the rather intimidating world of the
machine I was determined not to produce a dehumanised
work if I could help it, and so kept fairly close to the world
of the original sounds. The territory that the new computer
technology opens up is unprecedentedly vast: one is humbly
aware that it will only be conquered by penetration of the
human spirit, however beguiling the exhibits of technical
wizardry; and that penetration will neither be rapid or easy.'
Harvey's son was a chorister at Winchester Cathedral in the
1970s. The nine-minute work is based on the cathedral's
great tenor bell and the boy's voice, which join and separate with haunting ease. Inscribed on the bell are the words
Horas Avolantes Numero Mortuos Plango: Vivos ad Preces Voco
('I count the fleeting hours, I mourn the dead: I call the living to prayers'). The bell tolls its rich spectrum for the dead.
The boy represents the living. Harvey, who had been a boy
chorister himself and later embraced Zen Buddhism, said of
the piece: 'The walls of the concert hall are conceived as the
sides of the bell inside which is the audience, and around
which flies the free spirit of the boy.'

'Ophelia's Song' (1983)

The catalogue overflows with sad songs. I have chosen one by Elizabeth Maconchy (1907–1994) to whom I owe a special debt. She was the subject of my first published article, in the *Guardian*. Had she not been game to let a novice waste her time (I knew how to start an interview but, as with skating, had no idea how to stop. It ran on for hours and included a long exploration of her Irish husband William LeFanu's family tree, going back to the playwright Richard Sheridan), this book probably would not exist. Maconchy was unflappable, measured, dismissive of the difficulties she faced as a woman composer. 'I wrote when the children were in bed,' she said, as if it were that easy. Years later, attempting to follow her lead, I wondered precisely what ploys she had used to keep them there. Her thirteen string quartets are models of economy, variety and feeling. So too is this short Shakespearean lament from *Hamlet*. It has the colours of a traditional ballad, with the refrain 'He is dead and gone, lady,/ He is dead and gone,/ At his head a grass-green turf,/ At his heels a stone.'

The slow movement of Schubert's String Quintet in C, indeed the entire work, travels the full, universal journey of grief and consolation. Little wonder it is a favourite choice on BBC Radio 4's *Desert Island Discs.* You could add, too, his string quartet 'Death and the Maiden'. Two works by Tallis, his *Miserere nostri* and the *Lamentations of Jeremiah,* Gesualdo's *Tenebrae* and Couperin's *Leçons de ténèbres* are masterworks of the genre. Mozart's *Maurerische Trauermusik (Masonic Funeral Music)*, Beethoven's *Funeral March* from the 'Eroica', Chopin's *Marche funèbre* from the B flat minor Sonata and John Tavener's *Funeral Ikos* offer sober comfort. Shostakovich's 'Babi Yar' Symphony is an outpouring of anguish. Ravel's *Pavane pour une infante défunte,* Holst's *A Dirge for Two Veterans,* Arvo Pärt's *Cantus in memoriam Benjamin Britten* and Harrison Birtwistle's *Tombeau in memoriam Igor Stravinsky* have specific focus. You could fill a book with requiems. Medieval, Renaissance and Baroque music, so closely dependent on church liturgy, is replete with them: try Ockeghem, then Victoria, then Marc-Antoine Charpentier. Later preferences include Brahms's *A German Requiem* and those by Berlioz, Verdi and Bruckner. Stravinsky's *Symphony of Psalms* and his late *Requiem Canticles* are powerful, without a shred of sentiment. Delius, Howells, Hindemith, Henze, Penderecki, Schnittke, Ligeti, John Rutter, Bernd Alois Zimmermann, Elena Firsova, Jocelyn Pook: the requiems list goes on. In addition to those by Mozart and Britten, listed elsewhere, my choice would be Fauré's. He noted, 'It has been said that my Requiem does not express the fear of death, and someone has called it a lullaby of death. But it is thus that I see death: as a happy deliverance, an aspiration towards happiness above, rather than as a painful experience.'

10

TIME PASSING

My life is light, waiting for the death wind,
Like a feather on the back of my hand.

T. S. ELIOT, 'Song of Simeon'

ORLANDE DE LASSUS

Lagrime di San Pietro (Tears of St Peter) (1594)

This hour-long work, exploring the stages of grief, is also a meditation on old age and sickness, tinged with irony. Once famous, but today still relatively obscure, Lassus (c. 1532–1594) is gaining admiration once more. The Franco-Flemish composer's reputation in his lifetime was so widespread that his name appears as Roland de Lassus, Orlande de Lassus, Orlandus Lassus, Roland de Lattre and Orlando di Lasso. Palestrina, his near contemporary, has always been better known, in part because he worked at the Vatican. It was Palestrina's name that surfaced in the nineteenth century when Romantic composers – notably Brahms – grew interested in the 'old music' of the Renaissance. Lassus's prolific output is more startling, less mellifluous, full of cryptograms, jokes, puns and arcane numerological secrets. The *Lagrime* – a cycle of twenty spiritual madrigals and a motet – was his last published work. With a depressive turn of mind and already ill, enduring hallucinations and insomnia, Lassus completed these blistering laments with a dedication to Pope Clement VIII dated 25 May 1594. Within weeks Lassus was dead. He left more than three thousand compositions. If you try only one, let it be the *Lagrime di San Pietro*.

Piano Sonata in B flat major (D. 960) (1828)

By 1828 Schubert's syphilis, diagnosed five years earlier, was growing more acute, yet this, his final year, was a time of febrile industry. In addition to the masterly C major String Quintet and more, he wrote three ambitious piano sonatas, intended as a triptych and completed in the weeks leading up to his death on 19 November. The B flat is the last and, at around forty-five minutes, the longest. The bittersweet opening melody, unhurried and rapturous, seems infinite, as if bar lines and pulse have evaporated, time no more urgent than a careless breeze dispersing the downy filaments of a dandelion clock. The second movement is more brooding, the third delicate and lithe, the last a quixotic, mostly smiling rondo that pauses and revs up again. The regret of thinking it's over at once turns to relief, knowing there's still a twist and a turn to go. Anton Diabelli – lucky recipient of Beethoven's variations on a little waltz the publisher-composer had written – eventually printed an edition of the three sonatas in 1839, taking it upon himself to dedicate them to Schumann, Schubert's faithful (posthumous) champion. Schumann declared the ending of the B flat major Sonata cheerful and optimistic, concluding that the young Viennese composer, dead at thirty-one, had faced his end 'with a serene countenance'.

ROBERT SCHUMANN

Theme and Variations in E flat major (*Geistervariationen*, 'Ghost Variations') (1854)

This is music of a broken spirit, sapped of colour yet struggling to find fragile expression. In the asylum at Endenich, on the outskirts of Bonn, where he spent the last two years of his life, Robert Schumann believed he heard music dictated to him by angel voices. He began to write his Theme and Variations in E flat, the 'Ghost Variations', one of his final compositions. The instructions *leise und innig* are marked at the start; 'gentle and heartfelt'. If a psychiatrist said that this work, or its maker, showed signs of clinical depression, it would be a fair assessment. In the middle of writing it, on 4 March 1854, Schumann threw himself, half dressed, into the Rhine in a suicide attempt. The handwriting in the last variation differs from what had gone before; perhaps he returned to the work after trying to drown himself. His mental and physical state deteriorated further until his death in 1856. His wife Clara, and his loyal friend Brahms, destroyed some of the music from this period, fearing they would show an unbalanced mind. Brahms, saving the E flat 'Ghost' theme, wrote his own set of variations, as if trying to salvage something from the wrecked composer's final days. After years of neglect, considered unperformable in their strangeness, the *Geistervariationen* – Schumann's last utterances – are now played more often. This short offering has an air of distilled sanity, a ghost of genius present behind every bar.

Four Last Songs (1948)

'Is this perhaps death?' ask the weary old couple looking into the evening glow in Eichendorff's poem 'Im Abendrot' ('In the Sunset'). Richard Strauss, exiled in Switzerland awaiting de-Nazification (a decision was made in his favour before he died), had noted down the text in his sketchbook of 1946. It was the first of his 'four last' orchestral songs – his publisher chose the collective title – eventually completed two years later. He and his wife, Pauline, the operatic soprano who had inspired so much of his work as well as engendering his love of the female voice, were in their eighties. Their relationship was stormy but intense and devoted. He acknowledged adoringly that she was coquettish, difficult, complex, perverse, fickle and 'at every minute different from how she had been a moment before'.

Strauss chose three other poems, by Hermann Hesse: the ecstatic 'Frühling' ('Spring'), the dreamlike 'Beim Schlafengehen' ('When Falling Asleep'), with its death-wish cry, and 'September', which ends with an image of summer closing its eyes for winter. Fittingly Strauss died in that month, on 8 September 1949, a fifth song unfinished on his desk. The Swedish soprano Kirsten Flagstad gave the premiere, eight months after the composer's death and nine days after Pauline's, in May 1950. Acceptance, regret, passion and redemption well up in each bar of these light-suffused works, a sublime farewell to a long life.

String Quartet No. 3, Op. 94 (1975)

'What seemed to him so hard to bear', Thomas Mann wrote in *Death in Venice*, was 'the notion that he would never again set eyes on Venice, that this would be a permanent farewell'. Benjamin Britten had written his opera on the novella two years earlier. Now in poor health, he made his last journey to La Serenissima in November 1975, just before his sixty-second birthday. He stayed at the Danieli, as had Wagner, Mendelssohn and Debussy before him. From the hotel balcony, Britten could see across to La Salute, star-shaped and domed, rising out of the lagoon at the mouth of the Grand Canal. That church was built in homage to the Madonna 'of health' in thanks for deliverance from plague. Britten's 'plague' was heart disease. He had already written the first four movements of his String Quartet No. 3. He knew time was short. He had neglected the medium for three decades: his previous quartet had been premiered in 1945 to mark the 250th anniversary of Purcell's death. The Third Quartet is spare, serene, luminous. Despite exhaustion, Britten completed the finale of the quartet on his last day in Venice. He called this last movement *Recitative and Passacaglia*, built on a repeated bass figure, 'La Serenissima'. The instrumental lines spin around each other, fine and delicate but with the tensile strength of silk. Britten died in Suffolk in December 1976. He missed by a fortnight the quartet's world premiere, in Snape Maltings played by the Amadeus Quartet. These old friends had, however, given him a private performance shortly before his death.

ELLIOTT CARTER

Dialogues II (2012)

At the age of a hundred and three, Elliott Carter (1908–2012) wrote a short piece – one of many in his centenarian years – for piano and chamber orchestra for his friend Daniel Barenboim's birthday. How youthful Barenboim must have felt, to have reached his own three score years and ten only to receive a gift from someone nearly half as old again. The last premiere in Carter's lifetime, it was first performed on 25 October 2012 at La Scala, Milan, with Barenboim as soloist and Gustavo Dudamel, little more than a third the composer's age, as conductor. Less than a fortnight later Carter died in New York, the city of his birth. *Dialogues II* opens with piano cascades spliced with brass, wind and string chords. Then a short toccata leads to a big dissonance promising crisis. Instead, after a few hammered notes and a throwaway flourish, it ends, snuffed out with a grin. Carter was lucky to escape many of the worst indignities of old age. His close friends Carol Archer (*see left*) and her husband, the cellist Fred Sherry, dedicatee of several Carter works, saw the composer daily in his last year. Before an operation to correct the composer's heart arrhythmia, Carol recalls looking at the heart monitor with Carter: 'After it was over, the doctor showed it to us again. Elliott turned to me and said: "Look! Before I was beating like Stravinsky, and now I'm beating like Bach!"' He was, of course, beating like Elliott Carter, one of the great musical voices of the twentieth century, who defied the odds and spilled over into the twenty-first.

'Abendempfindung' (1787)

Mozart wrote 'Evening Thoughts' in June 1787, after *The Marriage of Figaro*, around the time of *Eine kleine Nachtmusik* and between the two great string quintets, in C major and G minor. The manuscript is in the British Library, London, part of the collection of Stefan Zweig. It speaks to friends or loved ones of a premonition of death. Dedicated to Laura, or Lana, it ended up in several Viennese Masonic song books. It does not need close analysis. The tragic mood is clear. The sun has gone. Life, too, is soon over, our revels ended. Do not be shy to shed a tear: 'It will be the finest pearl in my diadem.' Mozart's songs are relatively unfamiliar to most of us. I heard this live for the first time in 2015 performed by soprano Felicity Lott and pianist Graham Johnson at the funeral of a great Mozartian, Claus Moser, a man of the world – in the arts, business, politics – who lived for music.

Whether long lived or cut down young, knowing the end was nigh or dying unexpectedly, every composer has late and last works. We risk romanticising their place in the rest of the oeuvre: how can we not? Pergolesi was suffering from tuberculosis when he wrote his beautiful *Stabat Mater* in the last weeks of his life. He died aged twenty-six. The Spanish composer Arriaga wrote his dazzling Symphony in D when he was seventeen and was dead two years later. Handel struggled with his last oratorio, *Jephtha*, with blindness all but defeating him. The 'Et incarnatus est' from the *B minor Mass* was one of Bach's final works, but a week before his death, blind and having suffered a stroke, he was working on the chorale *Vor deinen Thron tret'ich hiermit* ('Before your throne I now appear'). Haydn's Piano Sonata in E flat major (HXVI:52), his final one, erupts with joy, light and shade. Beethoven's extraordinary late works – not least the piano sonatas and string quartets – are a subject in their own right. In his Op. 63 Mazurkas, Chopin squeezes every ounce of artistry into these late endeavours. So, too, Brahms in his two Clarinet Sonatas, Op. 120 (also arranged for viola). Verdi completed the *Te Deum* and *Stabat Mater* of his Four Sacred Pieces after that 'late masterpiece' *Falstaff*. Elgar wrote his *Dream of Gerontius*, about old age and death, in midlife. Four late works by the same composer are among his greatest: the Violin Sonata, String Quartet, Piano Quintet and Cello Concerto, all incidentally, except the quintet, in the key of E minor. Richard Strauss found high spirits in his wonderful Sonatina in F major, 'From a Convalescent's Workshop', for woodwind. Tippett's *Rose Lake*, Messiaen's *Éclairs sur l'au-delà* and Lutosławski's Fourth Symphony share that visionary gleam and grandeur of the long distant view from old age.

AND YET . . . UNFINISHED WORKS

You'll find its outline in my drawer,
Down below, with the unfinished business;
I didn't have the time to write it out, which is a shame,
It would have been a fundamental work.

PRIMO LEVI: 'Unfinished Business', translated
by Jonathan Galassi

JOHANN SEBASTIAN BACH

The Art of Fugue (1748)

Fourteen fugues and four canons in the key of D minor sounds a pedantic way to define one of the greatest achievements in the pinnacles of Western art. (All too dangerously close to 'forty teeth' and 'twelve incisive' to describe the mouth of Gradgrind's horse in Dickens's *Hard Times.*) It at least has the merit of accuracy. Little is known about Bach's intentions. Some scholar-performers argue that *The Art of Fugue* was written for keyboard. Others counter by saying some parts are unplayable on a keyboard and therefore it was intended for unspecified instruments. Great mystery surrounds the last section. Bach left the last fugue unfinished, breaking off at the point where he introduces a theme on his own name. His son, Carl Philipp Emanuel Bach, wrote on the manuscript that at this point, 'The composer died.'

Until writing this entry I had accepted this slightly honeyed version of events. Surely the man's son would know. A performance that ends mid-bar, instead of using one of the many attempted completions, makes a startling impact. The truth is all the more intriguing. Since the manuscript is written in Bach's own hand, experts conclude he must have finished it at least a year earlier (1748) when his health and eyesight were good enough. We know, too, that Bach was organising the engraving of it, without having completed the final quadruple fugue. Did he give up? Was it a cryptic joke, or a superstition that bringing it to a conclusion might invite his own end? We can only wonder.

String Quartet in D minor, Op. 103 (1803)

Self-effacing yet proud, Haydn fought against the travails of a weakening body with all his might. In his final decade he always took care over his appearance, with cane, hat, gloves and signet ring giving him a raffish air. Card games, books, visits from friends and admiring younger musicians kept him occupied, staving off melancholy. Haydn suffered from arteriosclerosis, causing swollen legs and difficulty in walking. He was taken twice to the Servite church in Vienna to pray at the shrine of St Peregrine, patron saint of bad legs. Quoting one of his own song settings, he had the words 'Hin ist alle meine Kraft, und schwach bin ich' ('With all my strength gone, I am weak') somewhat mawkishly print-ed on his visiting card. Those words, at his request, were also inscribed on the two inner movements of his final string quartet: not a farewell but a burning, intense tussle with new harmonic ideas of almost shocking boldness. The soulful *Andante* shifts invisibly to distant keys, ending with a falling, yearning melody and a sudden eruption, as if to say, 'I will go on.' The *Minuet* tears off with madcap energy, off-beat rhythms, turbulent climactic moments and a tum-bling first violin phrase across three octaves. These are new horizons for a composer nearing his end. After three years of effort, the surviving sketches rutted with crossings out, Haydn gave up. The string quartet form was both starting point and end of his career as a composer. This torso would be his mesmerising farewell.

WOLFGANG AMADEUS MOZART

Requiem (1791)

Myth and intrigue surround the writing of Mozart's Requiem: a mysterious visitor, an anonymous commission, an unsigned letter, the composer's own fear – according to a report in a Salzburg newspaper published a month after his death – that he was working 'with tears in his eyes' on what he believed would be his own requiem. So it proved. The Mass was far from complete when Mozart died, just after midnight on 5 December 1791, aged thirty-five. Only the opening *Requiem aeternam* was fully finished. Much of the *Kyrie*, the *Dies irae* and other sections were nearly done, but the wonderful *Lacrymosa* ended after eight bars and large holes were left elsewhere. Rumours and counter-rumours flew, in part set in motion by Mozart's wife Constanze for fear that payment would not be made if the work was known to be unfinished. All these tales furnished Peter Shaffer with a sinister ending to his play *Amadeus*. There is no doubt that other hands – chiefly those of Franz Xaver Süssmayr – completed the manuscript, a mix of reconstruction, reinvention, half-remembered conversation, error and guesswork. This poses an age-old problem. How closely do we associate a work of art we love with its maker? Should we stop listening the moment the *Lacrymosa* starts, knowing that what follows is not 'fully authentic Mozart'? It has not troubled performers. There are at least 45 recordings. After trying them one by one, you might or might not reach a conclusion. The question dangles in perpetuity. The music holds us in its grip.

FRANZ SCHUBERT

Symphony No. 8 in B minor ('Unfinished' (1822)

So much about Schubert is enigmatic, this piece above all. What made him, after completing two glorious movements and twenty bars of a third, put his pen down and leave his Symphony No. 8 unfinished? He had begun orchestrating the work at the end of October 1822, having already made extensive piano sketches for three movements. If there was a finale, nothing is known about it. Ever insecure when it came to his abilities, Schubert might have despaired that the rest of the piece could not match the genius of the first two parts – one theory among scholars. It is known that he was overwhelmed by the example of Beethoven, whom he hero-worshipped. Illness could have been the cause. This was the year Schubert fell ill with the syphilis that would darken the remaining six years of his life, causing bouts of sickness and depression. He sent the manuscript to his friend Anselm Hüttenbrener – a composer, one-time pupil of Salieri and friend of Beethoven – who kept it under wraps until its first performance in 1865, nearly four decades after its composition. That posthumous discovery made it appear, to one nineteenth-century critic, that Schubert was 'composing invisibly' from beyond the grave. With its uninhibited melodies, from that first clarinet and oboe song floating over trembling violins, its long lines and visionary scale, its pathos and shadows, the 'Unfinished' might indeed be reaching out to beyond.

ANTON BRUCKNER

Symphony No. 9 in D minor (1887–94)

'I don't want to start the Ninth at all. I lack courage – for Beethoven's Ninth also marked the end of his life.' Bruckner was superstitious with reason. Suffering from cirrhosis of the liver, diabetes and depression, staggering on swollen limbs up the six flights of stairs to his apartment, he worked on his Ninth Symphony until the day of his death. He dedicated it to 'the beloved God', and when a friend suggested he write his own requiem, responded that he had, in this work, already done so. As Bruckner left the work unfinished, it is usually played in the completed three movements. Extensive sketches of the *Finale*, amounting to some 600 bars, have prompted at least seven completions. What survives suggests a chorale, a fugue and a hopeful echo of the German Easter hymn 'Christ ist erstanden' ('Christ is risen'). In 2012 Simon Rattle recorded a new version by a team of four Brucknerians, convincing to many. Rattle said at the time, 'With this *Finale* you can still tell that in some ways it is a sketch, but there is so much of vintage Bruckner in it . . . Of course, this cannot be exactly what Bruckner finally would have offered to the world, but we can now hear the symphony as a really complete work'. He concluded: 'It has definitely changed my perception if not the conception of the whole work.' The story is still unfolding.

GUSTAV MAHLER

Symphony No. 10 (1910)

In 1910, the terrible last summer of his life, unwell and suffering from the knowledge that his wife Alma was having
an affair with the architect Walter Gropius, Mahler worked
frantically on his Tenth Symphony. He left 72 pages of full
score, 50 pages of short (not orchestrated) score and 44 further pages of sketches at his death, aged fifty, the following
spring. The final movement is inscribed with an impassioned outburst of love for Alma: 'Für dich leben! Für dich
stern! Almschi!' ('To live for you! To die for you! Almschi!').
If the story of this work's composition is dramatic, the tale
of its reconstruction is one of struggle, devotion and discovery. In 1924 Alma unexpectedly allowed two movements of
the symphony to be performed. 'The walls erected here are
unfinished, scaffolding conceals the building and yet the plan
and proportions can be clearly discerned,' she said. Debates
raged about the niceties of performing it incomplete. No one
attempted completing it until the 1950s. (Both Schoenberg
and Shostakovich refused.) The authoritative performing
version is that by the musicologist Deryck Cooke, aided by
British composers David Matthews and Colin Matthews.
Be astonished by the radical harmonies of the *Adagio*, the
rhythmic inventions of the *Scherzo*, the wild madness of the
Purgatorio and unnamed fourth movement, and the capa-
cious pulling together of ideas in the *Finale*. To hear this is
to understand the previous nine symphonies in a new light
and to glimpse Mahler's fresh ambitions.

This is not about the scraps and sketches that were barely begun, but those ambitious compositions left tantalisingly close to completion: named, identified, in sight of the finishing line. The canon of literature (not to mention all art forms) has many examples of the unfinished: Thucydides' *History of the Peloponnesian Wars*, Chaucer's *The Canterbury Tales*, Spenser's *The Faerie Queene* (probably long enough as it is), Dickens's *The Mystery of Edwin Drood*. Music left mid-bar is more difficult: Puccini's *Turandot* has had many 'finishers', but Toscanini, conducting the world premiere in 1926, two years after Puccini's death, laid down his baton at the point the original score ended. Opera is littered with the nearly-but-not-quites: Mussorgsky's *Khovanshchina*, Berg's *Lulu*, Schoenberg's *Moses und Aron*. Schoenberg's oratorio *Die Jakobsleiter* has been performed incomplete. Britten's last pronouncement, the fragment *Praise We Great Men*, was edited and orchestrated by Colin Matthews for performance. There are many more symphonies: Beethoven's Tenth ('completed' by Barry Cooper), a symphony in E flat by Tchaikovsky that became part of his Piano Concerto No. 3, incomplete at the time of his death. Bartók was 17 bars from the end of his Piano Concerto No. 3 (completed by his friend Tibor Serly). The quest for Sibelius's 'lost' Eighth Symphony continues. The most significant 'completion' in recent times has been Elgar's Third Symphony, 'elaborated' by the composer Anthony Payne. I have a special fondness for this. When I worked as music editor at the *Independent*, Tony was one of the best music critics. I knew, vaguely, that he was working on Elgar sketches. Eventually the first performance was given, by the BBC Symphony Orchestra in 1998, and an unfinished finished symphony joined the repertoire.

Last Word

LUDWIG VAN BEETHOVEN

String Quartet in F major, Op. 135 (1826)

The final entry was never in doubt. Bach is the perpetual spring, giving life to all music that came after, 'the immortal God of harmony', as Beethoven called him. Beethoven in turn is the torrential river, forging forward to the open sea, changing the landscape for ever. For Schubert, Brahms, Mahler, Bruckner and countless since, Beethoven was the touchstone, the God not of harmony but of harmonic instability and change, radical invention and startling fantasy. Chopin and many others resisted him. 'He is not human,' concluded Berlioz, fighting at first then yielding. Beethoven could have dominated this entire list: a towering choral masterpiece, nine symphonies, thirty-two piano sonatas, sixteen string quartets, seven concertos, the 'Ghost' and 'Archduke' piano trios alone, miraculous in variety. It would have to be all, or (very nearly) nothing.

Midway through writing, I interviewed Bernard Haitink, eighty-six and still busy. Off the podium he devours recordings of music he cannot conduct. 'Beethoven. I come back always to Beethoven, piano music, chamber music. Why? Because Beethoven is the consoler. The *great* consoler.' The description struck home. Beethoven's last string quartet, Op. 135, written in the autumn of 1826, is almost modest compared with the other 'late' quartets. The opening movements are lean, conversational, lyrical. The tranquil slow movement, with its moments of near stasis, commands us to stop all else. The finale reveals Beethoven's own struggle, musical or otherwise: he wrote in the score 'Muss es sein? Es muss sein!' ('Must it be? It must be!') Spirited, occasionally argumentative, at times ironic, serene, wise and full of jokes, this is the best of humanity. This is the best it gets. This is music to carry us through.

Epilogue

At that hour when all things have repose,
O lonely watcher of the skies,
Do you hear the night wind and the sighs
Of harps playing unto Love to unclose
The pale gates of sunrise?

When all things repose, do you alone
Awake to hear the sweet harps play
To Love before him on his way,
And the night wind answering in antiphon
Till night is overgone?

Play on, invisible harps, unto Love,
Whose way in heaven is aglow
At that hour when soft lights come and go,
Soft sweet music in the air above
And in the earth below.

JAMES JOYCE, 'Chamber Music III'

Suggested Listening

An informal and undogmatic guide to performers and recordings.
Also listen: www.fionamaddocks.co.uk/musicforlife

1 Childhood, Youth

- Pérotin Alleluia Nativitas: the Hilliard Ensemble's pioneering disc remains a top choice (ECM).
- Mozart Twelve Variations on 'Ah vous dirai-je, Maman': from many on offer, Walter Gieseking's on EMI Références is a classic.
- Schumann *Abegg Variations*: choose from Lang Lang, Evgeny Kissin or Imogen Cooper to late greats Claudio Arrau, Sviatoslav Richter and Clara Haskil.
- Bizet *Jeux d'enfants*: the Labèque sisters are ideal for Gallic authenticity and shared memories.
- Mendelssohn Octet: try ensembles such as the Melos or the Nash, or collaborations between two quartets (as in the Brandis Quartett and Westphal-Quartett on DG). Star violinists (Daniel Hope, James Ehnes, Christian Tetzlaff, Pinchas Zukerman) all have much to offer.
- Rachmaninoff Piano Concerto No. 1: Leif Ove Andsnes (soloist) with the Berliner Philharmoniker, conductor Antonio Pappano (Warner) leads in a big field. Pianists Denis Matsuev, Simon Trpčeski, Stephen Hough and Krystian Zimerman are excellent too.
- Claude Vivier *Lonely Child*: Montreal Postmoderne (CMC).
- Falla 'Nana': included in *Siete canciones populares españolas* (traditional; arranged by Manuel de Falla). sung by Bernarda Fink (piano, Anthony Spiri) (Harmonia Mundi).

- Vivaldi 'La tempesta di mare' (RV253): Andrew Manze and the Academy of Ancient Music offer a breezy account in *Vivaldi: Concert for the Prince of Poland* (Harmonia Mundi).
- Rameau Overture to *Zaïs*: Christophe Rousset and Les Talens Lyriques are experts, in *Overtures* (Decca L'Oiseau Lyre), or the whole of *Zaïs* (Aparté).
- Wagner *Der fliegende Holländer* (*The Flying Dutchman*): top Wagnerian conductors include Georg Solti, Daniel Barenboim, James Levine. Marek Janowski's recent issue with the Berlin Rundfunk chorus and orchestra is recommended. Many budget or mid-price sets are available.
- Debussy *La Mer*: Bernard Haitink conducting the Royal Concertgebouw Orchestra (Decca), Stéphane Denève with the Royal Scottish National (Chandos), Simon Rattle with the Berliner Philharmoniker or Mark Elder with the Hallé: all suitably briny.
- Butterworth *Bredon Hill*: Roderick Williams (baritone) with Iain Burnside (piano) – matchless (Naxos).
- Holst *Egdon Heath*: Andrew Davis conducting the BBC Symphony Orchestra (Apex) or Richard Hickox with the London Symphony Orchestra (Chandos).
- Sibelius *Tapiola*: great Sibelians include Colin Davis, Osmo Vänskä, Paavo Järvi or Vladimir Ashkenazy.
- Tippett 'Ritual Dances' from *The Midsummer Marriage*: Richard Hickox conducting the BBC National Orchestra of Wales (Chandos), paired with Tippett's late *The Rose Lake*.
- Messiaen *Des canyons aux étoiles*: for authenticity try an older recording with the composer's wife Yvonne Loriod on piano. The London Philharmonic Orchestra's live 2013 recording, conducted by Christoph Eschenbach, is vivid (LPO).
- Harrison Birtwistle *Silbury Air*: expertly played by his

long-term exponents, the London Sinfonietta, conducted by
Elgar Howarth (NMC).

- Peter Sculthorpe *Kakadu*: part of a showcase of his music
  recorded by the Queensland Orchestra, conductor Michael
  Christie (ABC Classics).

3 *Alive, Overflowing*

- Handel *Arrival of the Queen of Sheba*: included on mezzo
  soprano Sarah Connolly's *Heroes and Heroines*, with Harry
  Christophers and The Sixteen (Coro). Or in its original
  setting: *Solomon* performed by Paul McCreesh and the Gabrieli
  Consort and Players (Archiv).
- Bach *Singet dem Herrn ein neues Lied* (BWV 225): plenty of
  good ones around but the Monteverdi Choir and John Eliot
  Gardiner (Bach Motets, SDG) outshine most.
- Mozart Serenade in B flat major (K. 361) 'Gran Partita': a long
  work needing agility and energy. The London Winds with
  Michael Collins (Onyx) or the Linos Ensemble (Capriccio)
  deliver both.
- Beethoven Symphony No. 8 in F: from a huge field steer
  towards conductors such as Riccardo Chailly, Mariss Jansons,
  Nikolaus Harnoncourt, Bernard Haitink, John Eliot Gardiner.
- Schubert 'Trout' Quintet: many feature star pianists such
  as Alfred Brendel, András Schiff, Paul Lewis or, going back,
  Clifford Curzon. Try a left-field pairing: Thomas Adès's
  Piano Quintet, with Adès on piano, and the Arditti Quartet
  (Warner). Supplement with the Barenboim, Du Pré et al. DVD
  (Christopher Nupen Films: A13CND).
- Brahms String Quintet No. 2 in G, Op. 111: the Takács
  Quartet with Lawrence Power, viola (Hyperion).
- Coleridge-Taylor Ballade in A minor, Op. 33: watch Wayne
  Marshall conducting Chineke! online.

- Elgar Serenade for Strings: BBC Symphony Orchestra and Andrew Davis pair it with *Enigma Variations* (Apex); Davis and the Philharmonia, with James Ehnes, offer Elgar's Violin Concerto (Onyx).
- Janáček Sinfonietta: any recording conducted by Charles Mackerras will be strong; or Edward Gardner's recent disc with the Bergen Philharmonic (Chandos), or the Prague Radio Symphony Orchestra with Tomáš Netopil (Supraphon).
- Rossini 'La Danza': Joyce DiDonato (mezzo), Antonio Pappano (piano), *Live at Wigmore Hall* (Erato).
- Steve Reich *Clapping Music: Early Works* (Nonesuch) has the composer performing. Otherwise try Pierre-Laurent Aimard (Teldec).

4 Change

- Dunstable *Veni Sancte Spiritus*: included on *The Merton Collection: Merton College at 750* (Delphian), For a concentrated Dunstable encounter – Orlando Consort, Hilliard Ensemble or Tonus Peregrinus.
- Bach Fantasia and Fugue in G minor (BWV 542) 'Great': Peter Hurford, Simon Preston, Ton Koopman, Christopher Herrick – all Bach authorities.
- Beethoven Piano Sonata in B flat major, 'Hammerklavier': from present to past, Igor Levit, Alessio Bax, François-Frédéric Guy; András Schiff, Daniel Barenboim, Alfred Brendel; Sviatoslav Richter, Emil Gilels, John Ogdon.
- Sibelius Symphony No. 3: conductors Colin Davis, Neemi Järvi, Osmö Vänskä, Simon Rattle - all good. The Lahti Symphony Orchestra with Okko Kamu (BIS) have won rave reviews.
- Schoenberg String Quartet No. 2: the Fred Sherry Quartet (Naxos) pair it with 6 A Cappella Folksongs for Mixed Chorus. The Brindisi Quartet and the LaSalle both

programme it with Webern and Berg.

- Stravinsky *The Rite of Spring*: Simon Rattle and the Berliner Philharmoniker (Warner), Teodor Currentzis and Music Aeterna (Sony), Andrés Orozco-Estrada and the Frankfurt Radio Symphony Orchestra (Pentatone) - all distinctive performances. Or savour Jean-Efflam Bavouzet and François-Frédéric Guy in the piano-duet version (Chandos).
- Florence Price Symphony in E Minor: Leslie B. Dunner conducting the New Black Music Repertory Ensemble (Albany).
- Cage Sonatas and Interludes: Antonis Anissegos (Wego), John Tilbury (Decca) or, incomplete but paired with sonatas by Domenico Scarlatti, David Greilsammer (Sony).
- Górecki *Totus Tuus*: Voces8, The Sixteen, Choir of King's College, Cambridge, Collegium Vocale, Holst Singers and more include this in mixed-repertoire discs. The Silesian Philharmonic Choir with Waldemar Sutryk pair it with Polish choral music (Dux).
- Boulez *Pli selon pli*: Ensemble InterContemporain with Christine Schäfer (soprano) and the composer as conductor (DG).
- Fauré 'Les Berceaux': from high to low, new and old, Véronique Gens, Sandrine Piau, Janet Baker, Ian Bostridge, Henk Neven, Gérard Souzay.

5 Love, Passion

- Machaut *Quant en moy*: the Orlando Consort are specialists in this repertoire (Hyperion).
- Monteverdi *Lamento della ninfa*: included on *Lamenti* (Erato), with Emmanuelle Haïm conducting Le Concert d'Astrée, with Natalie Dessay (soprano), Topi Lehtipuu (tenor) and Christopher Purves (bass).
- Barbara Strozzi *Sino alla morte*: appears on *A che Belleza!* – Renaissance arias and cantatas (Lindoro). Musica Secreta's

La virtuosissima cantatrice (Amon Ra) is devoted entirely to Strozzi's music.

- Liszt *Petrarch Sonnets*: Liszt masters include Alfred Brendel, Claudio Arrau, Georges Cziffra, Jorge Bolet, Lazar Berman. Newer entrants: Libor Nováček, Angela Hewitt, Yevgeny Sudbin and Llŷr Williams.

- Wagner Prelude to *Tristan und Isolde*: best to get the whole opera. Many classic performances are available at budget price. Stephen Gould and Nina Stemme with Marek Janowski (Pentatone), John Treleaven and Christine Brewer with Donald Runnicles (Warner), Siegfried Jerusalem and Waltraud Meier with Daniel Barenboim (Teldec) all reach the heights.

- Brahms Alto Rhapsody: made famous on disc first by Kathleen Ferrier, then by Janet Baker and Christa Ludwig. More recent options: Ann Hallenberg with Collegium Vocale Ghent, the Orchestre des Champs-Elysées and Philippe Herreweghe (PHI) or Nathalie Stutzmann with the Monteverdi Choir, the Orchestre Révolutionnaire et Romantique and John Eliot Gardiner (SDG).

- Tchaikovsky *Romeo and Juliet* Fantasy Overture: Russian National Orchestra with conductor Vladimir Jurowski, Russian National Orchestra with Mikhail Pletnev, RLPO with Vasily Petrenko, Kirov Orchestra with Valery Gergiev.

- Franck Violin Sonata in A major: James Ehnes (violin) and Andrew Armstrong (piano) scored high with their 2015 recording. (Onyx).

- Janáček String Quartets 1 and 2, 'The Kreutzer Sonata' and 'Intimate Letters': the Pavel Haas Quartet, the Jerusalem Quartet and the Dante Quartet each brings intensity.

- Britten Michelangelo Sonnet XXX: go for Peter Pears (tenor) with Britten as pianist (NMC). Or Mark Padmore with Iain Burnside (Signum), or Philip Langridge with Steuart Bedford (Naxos).

6 *Pause*

- Hildegard of Bingen *Columba aspexit*: the Gothic Voices' bestselling *Feather on the Breath of God* (Hyperion) remains a classic. Tarik O'Regan's *Columba aspexit* is included on a disc of English music by Wells Cathedral School Choralia (Naxos).
- Purcell's 'Complete Fantasias': superbly played by Fretwork (Harmonia Mundi). The Rose Consort of Viols and Phantasm are also recommended.
- Lili Boulanger *Vieille prière bouddhique*: the Monteverdi Choir, London Symphony Orchestra and conductor John Eliot Gardiner (DG) pair it with Stravinsky's *Symphony of Psalms*.
- Ligeti *Lontano*: the Wiener Philharmoniker–Claudio Abbado match it with Boulez, Nono and Rihm (DG). For more Ligeti try *The Ligeti Project* volumes 1–5 (Warner).
- Shostakovich 24 Preludes and Fugues: ideally you need two versions: the 1962 recording by Tatiana Nikolayeva (Doremi) and the 2010 one by Alexander Melnikov (Harmonia Mundi).
- Morton Feldman *Rothko Chapel*: part of a memorial concert in the Rothko chapel, Houston: *Rothko Chapel: Morton Feldman, Erik Satie, John Cage* (ECM).
- Schubert *Die schöne Müllerin*. Well over a hundred recordings exist. Baritone choices: Florian Boesch (piano, Malcolm Martineau), Christian Gerhaher (piano, Gerold Huber), Thomas Quasthoff (piano, Justus Zeyen) or the classic Dietrich Fischer-Dieskau–Gerald Moore partnership. Tenors: Jonas Kaufmann, Christoph Prégardien, Mark Padmore, Ian Bostridge . Higher or lower voices have tried it too.
- Stockhausen *Stimmung*: Gregory Rose and Singcircle (Hyperion) or Paul Hillier and Theatre of Voices (Harmonia Mundi) know how to handle it.
- Takemitsu *From me flows what you call Time*: Nexus (Sony) or the Berliner Philiharmoniker with Yutaka Sado on DVD. Or

find Andrew Davis–BBC Symphony Orchestra online.

- Arvo Pärt *Tabula Rasa*: violinists Gidon Kremer, Gil Shaham or Tasmin Little are fine advocates.

7 *War, Resistance*

- Dufay *L'homme armé*: Oxford Camerata, director Jeremy Summerly (Naxos) deliver it unadorned.
- Haydn *Missa in Angustiis* in D minor, the 'Nelson' Mass: Concentus Musicus Wien with Nikolaus Harnoncourt (Warner), Collegium Musicum 90 with Richard Hickox (Chandos) or the Oregon Bach Choir and Orchestra with Helmuth Rilling (Hänssler) stand out from the crowd.
- Chopin Etude in C minor, Op. 10 No. 12 ('Revolutionary'): a young man's work. Jan Lisiecki (DG) or Maurizio Pollini's 1960 recording (Testament) have youthful passion. But no need to stop there . . .
- Ravel *Le Tombeau de Couperin* requires a special lightness and brilliance: Jean-Efflam Bavouzet (MDG), Louis Lortie (Chandos), Steven Osborne (Hyperion), Alexandre Tharaud (Harmonia Mundi), Anne Queffélec (Erato), Pascal Rogé (Decca) all have it.
- Messiaen *Quatuor pour la fin du temps* (*Quartet for the End of Time*): the composer, and his wife Yvonne Loriod, recorded the work. Of modern readings, try the Hebrides Ensemble (Linn) or Gil Shaham and friends (DG).
- Shostakovich Symphony No. 7 ('Leningrad'): the Russian National Orchestra with Paavo Järvi (Pentatone), Gergiev and the Kirov Orchestra St Petersburg (Decca). Or go back earlier to the Leningrad Philharmonic Orchestra with Evgeny Mravinsky (Urania) or the USSR Ministry of Culture Symphony Orchestra with Gennady Rozhdestvensky (Melodiya). Semyon Bychkov (Leningrad born) and the

WDR Sinfonie-Orchester Köln (Avie) is excellent. For all Shostakovich's symphonies the Royal Liverpool Philharmonic Orchestra with Vasily Petrenko (St Petersburg born) are first rate.

- Britten *War Requiem*: choose from the composer's own recording (Decca), Antonio Pappano and his forces of Santa Cecilia, Rome (Warner) or Gianandrea Noseda with the LSO (LSO Live).
- George Crumb's *Black Angels* inspired the Kronos Quartet to form. Hear them on Nonesuch.
- Debussy 'Noël des enfants' appears on Robin Tritschler's *Great War Songs* (Signum) album (piano, Malcolm Martineau). Véronique Gens (piano, Roger Vignoles) sings it on *Nuit d'étoiles* (Erato).

8 *Journeys, Exile*

- Byrd Three Latin Masses: Westminster Cathedral Choir (Hyperion), Cardinall's Musick (Presto) or the Tallis Scholars (Gimmell) – all authoritative performances.
- Scarlatti Sonata in D (K. 492): Trevor Pinnock on harpsichord (Linn) or David Greilsammer (see *Cage: Sonatas and Interludes*, Sony) or, bursting with Spanish clicks and turns, Yevgeny Sudbin (BIS).
- Chopin 24 Preludes: you may want more than one. Martha Argerich, Alexandre Tharaud, Daniil Trifonov, Krystian Zimerman, Friedrich Gulda, Maria João Pires, Maurizio Pollini are all top Chopin exponents. Not forgetting late greats: Cortot, Arrau, Horowitz, Michelangeli, Cherkassky.
- Rebecca Clarke Viola Sonata: Tabea Zimmermann (viola), with pianist Kirill Gerstein (Mirios).
- Varèse *Amériques*: go for the French–American combination of Pierre Boulez conducting the Chicago Symphony Orchestra.

- Gershwin *An American in Paris*: the New York Philharmonic under Leonard Bernstein – an evergreen classic (Sony).
- Rachmaninoff's Symphonic Dances: Berliner Philharmoniker with Simon Rattle (DG) or the Royal Concertgebouw Orchestra and Mariss Jansons (RCO Live) provide sonic dazzle. Emanuel Ax and Yefim Bronfman are fiery in the piano duet version (Sony).
- Bartók Concerto for Orchestra: the Budapest Festival Orchestra with Iván Fischer or the Hungarian National Philharmonic Orchestra with Zoltán Kocsis (Hungaraton) catch the Hungarian accent. Georg Solti's with the Chicago Symphony Orchestra (Decca) is a classic.
- Frederic Rzewski *Winnsboro Cotton Mill Blues*: pianist Ralph van Raat includes on his all-Rzewski disc (Naxos). The composer plays the two-piano version with Ursula Oppens (Music & Arts).
- Brahms 'Heimweh II' ('Homesickness'), Op. 63 No. 8: choose from bass-baritone Robert Holl (piano, Graham Johnson) (Hyperion), baritone Dietrich Fischer-Dieskau (piano, Jörg Demus) (DG), mezzo soprano Anne Sofie von Otter (piano, Bengt Forsberg) (DG), soprano Elly Ameling (piano, Dalton Baldwin) (Philips). Or track down the great mezzo Janet Baker (included on various compilations).

9 *Grief, Melancholy, Consolation*

- Dowland 'Flow My Tears': from Andreas Scholl to Iestyn Davies to Sting, many have recorded the song. For Dowland's complete *Lachrymae or Seaven Teares* choose Fretwork (Erato) or the Rose Consort of Viols (Amon Ra).
- Purcell *Music for the Funeral of Queen Mary*: the Collegium Vocale Choir and Orchestra with Philippe Herreweghe (Harmonia Mundi), one of the many available recordings.

- Bach Cantata 106: *Gottes Zeit ist die allerbeste Zeit (Actus Tragicus)*: try the Monteverdi Choir's Cantata series with John Eliot Gardiner (SDG). Otherwise Bach Collegium Japan with Masaaki Suzuki (BIS).
- Berlioz *Tristia*: SWR Vokalensemble Stuttgart with Sylvain Cambreling (Hänssler) perform it with Berlioz choral works. Pierre Boulez and the Cleveland (DG) offer Berlioz's *Symphonie fantastique.*
- Berg Violin Concerto: Antje Weithaas, Isabelle Faust, Arabella Steinbacher, Gil Shaham, Renaud Capuçon all excel. Further back: Christian Ferras, Ivry Gitlis, Louis Krasner, Joseph Szigeti.
- Richard Strauss *Metamorphosen*: in the version for 23 strings (rather than sextet) try Mariss Jansons and the Bavarian Radio Symphony Orchestra (Oehms). In the 1970s, Rudolf Kempe conducted the Dresden Staatskapelle in a heartfelt account.
- Poulenc *Stabat Mater*: plenty of choice. Try this newish one: Cappella Amsterdam, Estonian Philharmonic Chamber Choir and Estonian National Symphony Orchestra with Daniel Reuss (Harmonia Mundi).
- Puccini *Crisantemi*: best matched with Verdi's String Quartet. The Hagen Quartet (DG), Quartetto David (BIS) or Quartet di Cremona (Klanglogo) all oblige. Or choose the Signum Quartett (Capriccio) which offers Hugo Wolf's short Italian Serenade.
- Jonathan Harvey *Mortuos Plango, Vivos Voco*: available in a fascinating Boulez-conducted box set (*The Complete Erato Recordings*).
- Elizabeth Maconchy 'Ophelia's Song': touchingly sung by Caroline MacPhie (soprano) with Joseph Middleton (piano) (Stone Records).

- Lassus *Lagrime di San Pietro*: Ensemble Vocal Européen with Philippe Herreweghe (Harmonia Mundi), or Gallicantus, directed by Gabriel Crouch (Signum).
- Schubert Piano Sonata in B flat major (D. 960): András Schiff, Mitsuko Uchida, Paul Lewis, Alfred Brendel , Imogen Cooper, all formidable Schubertians.
- Schumann Theme with Variations in E Flat (*Geistervariationen*, 'Ghost Variations'): Andreas Staier, playing on an 1837 Erard piano (Harmonia Mundi), or András Schiff (ECM) – contrasting approaches.
- Richard Strauss Four Last Songs: Jessye Norman's with the Leipzig Gewandhaus and Kurt Masur (Philips), Nina Stemme with the Royal Opera House orchestra and Antonio Pappano (Warner), Anja Harteros, Dorothea Röschmann, Karita Mattila, Christine Brewer, Felicity Lott all excel. Elisabeth Schwarzkopf and Lisa Della Casa are legends in this repertoire.
- Britten String Quartet No. 3: the Endellion Quartet (Warner) perform it with Britten's other quartets.
- Elliott Carter *Dialogues II* is available only on the DVD of *Daniel Barenboim's 70th Birthday Concert* (DG), or online.
- Mozart's 'Abendempfindung' (K. 523): Mark Padmore with Kristian Bezuidenhout, fortepiano (Harmonia Mundi); Barbara Bonney, with pianist Geoffrey Parsons (Elatus); Christoph Prégardien, with pianist Michael Gees (Challenge Classics) – all good. Not forgetting Lorraine Hunt Lieberson, with pianist Peter Serkin (Harmonia Mundi).

11 And Yet . . . Unfinished Works

- Bach *Art of Fugue:* for keyboard, Pierre-Laurent Aimard (DG) or Angela Hewitt (Hyperion); for organ, Helmut Walcha

(Archiv) or Bernard Foccroulle (Ricercar); for viol consort: Phantasm (Simax) or Fretwork (Harmonia Mundi); for harpsichord: Davitt Moroney (Harmonia Mundi) or Martha Cook (Passacaille). There are also many mixed instrumental versions.

- Haydn String Quartet in D minor, Op. 103: the Maggini Quartet (Claudio) and Kodály Quartet (Naxos).
- Mozart Requiem: from an enormous field, the Dunedin Consort with John Butt (Linn), Bach Collegium Japan with Masaki Suzuki (BIS), Royal Amsterdam Concertgebouw with Mariss Jansons (RCO), Les Arts Florissants with William Christie (Erato), Handel & Haydn Society with Harry Christophers (CORO) – all strong performances.
- Schubert 'Unfinished' Symphony: from nearly three hundred listed, Claudio Abbado conducting the Vienna Philharmonic in 1978 (Audit), re-released after the conductor's death in 2014, remains ideal.
- Bruckner Ninth Symphony: Lucerne Festival Orchestra with Claudio Abbado (DG) or Bernard Haitink's recording with the London Symphony Orchestra (LSO Live) are unrivalled. Simon Rattle and the Berliner Philharmoniker have included the 'fourth movement' completion (Warner).
- Mahler Tenth Symphony: Pierre Boulez and the Cleveland Orchestra (DG).

Last Word

- Beethoven String Quartet in F major, Op. 135: for choice, the Takács Quartet (Decca). Belcea Quartet, Lindsay Quartet, Végh Quartet, Emerson Quartet, Vanbrugh Quartet – all are admirable.

Acknowledgements

Immeasurable thanks to the Faber team: Belinda Matthews, Kate Ward, Alex Kirby; and to Jill Burrows, Peter McAdie and Bronagh Woods. Thanks also to: Carol Archer, Iain Burnside, Simon Callow, Julia Cartwright, Alexandra Coghlan, Sarah Donaldson, Jane Ferguson, Megan Fishpool, Clive Gillinson, Samuel Johnstone, Arabella Cooper Maddocks, Flora Cooper Maddocks, Colin Matthews, Gerard McBurney, Andrew Mitchell, Tarik O'Regan, Lucy Shortis, Lyn Youngson. Tom Phillips made his archive freely available and always knew exactly what was needed, in word or image. Bayan Northcott scrutinised the list at a key moment. Alice Wood gave help and wisdom with pictures. Stephen Roe knew all the obscure answers. Carol McDaid read and re-read the text, supplied pictures and spotted stray commas. As for the rest, in the words of a song not included in this book, blame it on me.

PICTURE PERMISSIONS

From the Tom Phillips Postcard Archive:

pages 2, 6, 22 (Eastbourne, 1905), 36, 38 (The Handel Orchestra, Crystal Palace), 40, 52, 56, 60, 64, 76, 82, 86 (Eugène Ysaÿe), 88 (D. Mastroianni), 92, 102, 110 (Zeppelin wreck, East Anglia, 1917), 112, 126, 130 (Mallorca/Chopin), 134 (Brookyn Bridge, NYC), 144 (St Cecilia, Rome), 160, 174. 180 (Sagrada Familia, Barcelona c.1900), 185 (Beethoven's death mask)

p.   8 The Eight Step Sisters, Worthing Beach, Fox Photos/Getty Images
p. 10 Rachmaninoff, 1895, photo by Fine Art Images/Heritage Images/Getty Images
p. 12 Isamu Noguchi Foundation and Garden Museum, New York
p. 16 and p. 26 © Carol McDaid
p. 18 Venice c.1900. François Le Diascorn/Gamma-Rapho via Getty Images
p. 28 Midsummer fire © withGod, Shutterstock
p. 30 Bryce Canyon, photo by jekershner7/depositphotos.com
p. 32 Silbury Hill, © John Drews, http://thesilburyrevelation.com
p. 44 Allegro Films, © Reg Wilson/EMI

TEXT PERMISSIONS

Index of Works Cited